THE REAL READER'S QUARTERLY

# Slightly Foxed

'Return to Arcadia'

NO.34 SUMMER 2012

*Editors* Gail Pirkis and Hazel Wood
*Marketing and publicity* Stephanie Allen and Jennie Paterson
*Subscriptions* Alarys Gibson, Anna Kirk and Richard Conyngham

*Cover illustration:* Ed Kluz, 'The Silver Fox'

Ed Kluz was raised in the Yorkshire Dales and now lives in Brighton. He studied painting at the Winchester School of Art. He is a printmaker, illustrator, painter and designer, and finds inspiration in the historical objects, buildings, landscape and folklore of Britain. His eyes look into the past but his feet are firmly in the present: www.edkluz.co.uk.

*Design by Octavius Murray*

*Layout by Andrew Evans*

*Colophon and tailpiece by David Eccles*



Published by Slightly Foxed Limited
67 Dickinson Court
15 Brewhouse Yard
London ECIV 4JX

tel 020 7549 2121/2111
fax 0870 1991245
e-mail all@foxedquarterly.com
www.foxedquarterly.com

*Slightly Foxed* is published quarterly in early March, June, September and December
Annual subscription rates (4 issues)
UK £36; Europe £44; Rest of the World £48
Concessions are available for those aged 26 or under: please call the office
Single copies of this issue can be bought for £9 (UK), £11 (Europe) or £12 (Rest of the World)
Back issues are also available

ISBN 978-1-906562-38-0

*Printed and bound by Smith Settle, Yeadon, West Yorkshire*

# *Contents*

Ian Stephens, 'Backwater'

Our bookshop can obtain any of the books mentioned in this issue.
Slightly Foxed on Gloucester Road, 123 Gloucester Road,
London SW7 4TE, e-mail: enquiries@foxedbooks.com, tel: 020 7370 3503

# *From the Editors*

Summer: the season of literary festivals, and *Slightly Foxed* is on the road. Our travels began early with an appearance, with author and contributor Penelope Lively, at the Words by the Water Festival in Cumbria in early March. Later that month we were at Christ Church, Oxford, for the first in what we hope will be a regular series of *Slightly Foxed* talks on forgotten authors at the Oxford Literary Festival. This year the philosopher and critic John Gray delivered a brilliant and entertaining talk on the work of John Cowper Powys, arising from the piece he wrote in our spring issue, neatly placing Powys as 'an outdoor Proust'. On 14 June we'll be launching the summer issue at Mr B's cosy and very individual bookshop in Bath. And on Sunday 8 July we'll be appearing at the West Meon Literary Festival in Hampshire with our contributor and prize-winning biographer Maggie Fergusson.

Whew! Right from the start we'd planned to launch each issue with a visit to a different independent bookshop, but we never really envisaged this life of festival appearances. Nor indeed of appearances in the national press – like the handsome feature on *Slightly Foxed* and the Slightly Foxed Editions by Gaby Wood in the Weekend section of the Saturday *Telegraph* of 10 March. You can see it on their website, along with a short film showing a Slightly Foxed Edition being printed and bound at our wonderful printers, Smith Settle in Yorkshire: http://www.telegraph.co.uk/culture/books/9134248/Outfoxing-the-digital-revolution.html.

And on the subject of SFEs, the latest, and one of the most unusual, is *The Flame Trees of Thika,* Elspeth Huxley's classic account of her childhood time in East Africa just before the First World War (see p. 14). In 1913 British East Africa, as it was then known, was still a kind of Garden of Eden, a place for the recouping of lost fortunes for those, like Elspeth's parents, who hadn't managed things very well elsewhere. *Flame Trees* is an unforgettably vivid evocation of that small, dispersed society of early white settlers and of the untouched beauty of Africa, seen through the eyes of a solitary and self-sufficient small child.

On Saturday 10 November we'll be staging our own modest version of a literary festival – another *Slightly Foxed* Readers' Day at the Art Workers' Guild in Bloomsbury. Perhaps, in fact, the success of our first Readers' Day last November rested partly on the fact that it *wasn't* a literary festival. Having no publishers to please or books to hype, the *SF* contributors who spoke were free to talk about any literary subject that interested them, and a tremendously jolly day was had by all. We have an equally interesting line-up of speakers this year and tickets are available now, so if you plan to come do get in touch, as last year they sold out fast. The day costs £50, including delicious cakes at teatime provided by our contributor Frances Donnelly, and we think all those who came last year would agree that it's money well spent.

And finally, we were gratified by the response to our Young Writers' Competition, which produced an entertaining batch of entries in a rich variety of styles. Congratulations to the winner, Marie Wicks, whose piece appears on p. 64. Her choice of author was original and we felt she had deftly captured both the tone and the spirit of *SF*. Congratulations too to the runners-up, Fred Gifford and Emma Goode, whose pieces can be read on our website, www.foxedquarterly.com.

GAIL PIRKIS

HAZEL WOOD

# *Return to Arcadia*

ALBERTO MANGUEL

Several times, during a long life of reading, I've been tempted to write an autobiography based solely on the books that have counted for me. Someone once told me that it was customary for a Spanish nobleman to have his coat of arms engraved on his bedhead so that visitors might know who it was who lay in a sleep that might always be his last. Why then not be identified by my bedside favourites, which define and represent me better than any symbolic shield? If I ever indulged in such a vainglorious undertaking, a chapter, an early chapter, would be given over to *The Wind in the Willows*.

I can't remember when I first read *The Wind in the Willows*, since it is one of those books that seem to have been with me always, but it must have been very early on, when my room was in a cool, dark basement and the garden I played in boasted four tall palm trees and an old tortoise as their tutelary spirit. The geography of our books blends with the geography of our lives, and so, from the very beginning, Mole's meadows and Rat's river bank and Badger's woods seeped into my private landscapes, imbuing the cities I lived in and the places I visited with the same feelings of delight and comfort and adventure that sprang from those much-turned pages. In this sense, the books we love become our cartography.

---

Though there are many editions of Kenneth Grahame's *The Wind in the Willows* (1908) in print, we particularly like that published by Prentice Hall which contains E. H. Shepard's illustrations (Hb · 256pp · £15.95 · ISBN 9780684179575) and the Everyman edition, with illustrations by Arthur Rackham (Hb · 256pp · £10.99 · ISBN 9781857159233).

In 1888, John Ruskin gave a name to the casual conjunction between physical nature and strong human emotions. 'All violent feelings', he wrote, 'produce in us a falseness in all our impressions of external things, which I would generally characterize as the "Pathetic Fallacy".' Kenneth Grahame magnificently ignored the warning. The landscape of Cookham Dene on the Thames (where he lived and which he translated into the world of Mole and Rat, Badger and Toad) is, emotionally, the source and not the result of a view of the world that cannot be distinguished from the world itself. There may have been a time when the bucolic English landscape lay ignored and untouched by words, but since the earliest English poets the reality of it lies to a far greater extent in the ways in which it has been described than in its mere material existence. No reader of *The Wind in the Willows* can ever see Cookham Dene for the first time. After the last page, we are all old inhabitants for whom every nook and cranny is as familiar as the stains and cracks on our bedroom ceiling. There is nothing false in these impressions.

There are books that have (beyond the calm that comes with familiarity) an intrinsically quiet, soothing quality. *The Wind in the Willows* is such a book. Something in the choice of words and the rhythm of its sentences echoes the mood of the ancient landscape Grahame loved and knew so well. But the ease of his prose is deceptive. 'A sentence that is easy to read', he once said, 'may have been difficult to put together. Perhaps the greater the easiness in writing, the harder that task in composition. Writing is not easy: I need not tell you that. There is always a pleasure in the exercise; but, also, there is always an agony in the endeavour. If we make a formula of those two motives, I think we may define the process. It is, at its best, a pleasurable agony.'

And yet, *The Wind in the Willows* did not start out at that leisurely pace. It began as a story breathlessly told to Mouse (the nickname of Grahame's son, Alastair) during a crying fit on his fourth birthday, and was then continued by letter while Alastair was at the seaside with his governess in the summer of 1907. This first version (if we are to judge by the letters published by Grahame's widow Elspeth in 1944 under the title *First Whisper of 'The Wind in the Willows'*) had a pure bedtime story tone, a fast-paced cuteness mercifully absent from the finished version.

Green Bank Hotel
Falmouth
10th May 1907

My Darling Mouse
Have you heard about the Toad? He was never taken prisoner by brigands at all. It was all a horrid low trick of his. He wrote that letter himself – the letter saying that a hundred pounds must be put in the hollow tree. And he got out of the window early one morning, & went off to a town called Buggleton, & went to the Red Lion Hotel & there he found a party that had just motored down from London, & while they were having breakfast he went into the stable-yard & found their motor-car & went off in it without even saying Poop-poop! And now he has vanished & everyone is looking for him, including the police. I fear he is a bad low animal.

Goodbye, from
Your loving Daddy

Mouse, though plagued by health problems, was, by all accounts, a fearless boy, as undaunted by danger as Toad himself. His mother said that he never dreaded 'anything of a material nature'. As a small child, he loved to hear the wind blowing outside the house at night, and when asked if he minded sleeping alone in the nursery, he answered: 'Not if you'll go away and shut the door.' And when asked further if he wasn't afraid of being all alone in the dark, he said: 'Not if you'll put out the light.'

Years later, Mouse was killed in an unexplained accident (probably suicide) when he was an undergraduate at Oxford. For the reader, the intrusion of this tragedy into the story of the story surreptitiously turns *The Wind in the Willows* into an elegy. The tone now is of something recognizably dear but lost, alive in memory (in the memory, constantly renewed, of the reader), eternally youthful because prevented by death from growing old.

Offering the novel to the publisher Charles Scribner's Sons, Grahame described it as 'a book of youth, and so perhaps chiefly *for* youth and those who still keep the spirit of youth alive in them; of life, sunshine, running water, woodlands, dusty roads, winter firesides, free of problems, clear of the clash of sex, of life as it might fairly be supposed to be regarded by some of the wise, small things "that glide in grasses and rubble of woody wreck".'

And yet the youthfulness of the book seems overlaid with another feeling: of contentment that is not often of youth but of the time that comes later, after the restlessness and anxiety of the new are over and we settle down in our destined place. *The Wind in the Willows* begins with a departure, and with a search and a discovery, but it soon achieves an overwhelming sense of peace and happy satisfaction, of untroubled familiarity. We are at home in Grahame's book.

But Grahame's universe is not one of retirement or seclusion, of withdrawal from the world. On the contrary, it is one of time and space shared, of mirrored experience. From the very first pages, the reader discovers that *The Wind in the Willows* is a book about friendship, one of those English friendships that Borges once described by saying that they 'begin by precluding confidences and end by forgoing dialogue'. The theme of friendship runs through all our literatures. Like Achilles and Patroclus, David and Jonathan, Don Quixote and Sancho Panza, Ishmael and Queequeg, Sherlock Holmes and Watson, Rat and Mole reflect for each other discovered identities and contrasting views of the world. Each one asserts for the other the better, livelier part of his character; each encourages the other to be his finer, brighter self. Mole may be lost without Rat's guidance but, without Mole's adventurous spirit, Rat would remain withdrawn and far too removed from the world. Together they build Arcadia out of their common surroundings; *pace* Ruskin, their friendship defines the place that has defined them.

If *The Wind in the Willows* was a sounding-board for the places I lived in, it became, during my adolescence, also one for my relationships, and I remember wanting to live in a world with absolute friends like Rat and Mole. Not all friendships, I discovered, are of the same kind. While Rat and Mole's bonds are unimpeachably solid, their relationship equally balanced and unquestioned (and I was fortunate enough to have a couple of friendships of that particular kind), their relationship with Badger is more formal, more distanced – since we are in England, land of castes and classes, and Badger holds a social position that requires a respectful deference from others. (Of the Badger sort, too, I found friends whom I loved dearly but with whom I always had to tread carefully, not wanting to be considered overbearing or unworthy.)

With Toad, the relationship is more troubling. Rat and Mole love Toad and care for him, and assist him almost beyond the obligations of affection, in spite of the justified exasperation he provokes in them. He, on the other hand, is far less generous and obliging, calling on

them only when in need or merely to show off. (Friends like Toad I also had, and these were the most difficult to please, the hardest to keep on loving, the ones that, over and over again, made me want to break up the relationship; but then they'd ask for help once more and once more I'd forgive them.)

Toad is the reckless adventurer, the loner, the eternal adolescent. Mole and Rat begin the book in an adolescent spirit but grow in wisdom as they grow in experience; for Toad every outing is a never-ending return to the same whimsical deeds and the same irresponsible exploits. If we, the readers, love Toad (though I don't) we love him as spectators; we love his clownish performance on a stage of his own devising and follow his misadventures as we follow those of a charming rogue.

But Mole and Rat, and even Badger, we love as our fellow creatures, equal to us in joy and in suffering. Badger is everyone's older brother; Rat and Mole, the friends who walk together and mature together in their friendship. They are our contemporaries, reborn with every new generation. We feel for their misfortunes and rejoice in their triumphs as we feel and rejoice for our nearest and dearest. During my late childhood and adolescence, their companionship was for me the model relationship, and I longed to share their *déjeuners sur l'herbe*, and to be part of their easy *complicité* as other readers long for the love of Mathilde or the adventurous travels of Sinbad.

*The Wind in the Willows* cannot be classed as a work of pure fantasy. Grahame succeeds in making his creatures utterly believable to us. The menageries of Aesop or La Fontaine, Günter Grass or Colette, Orwell or Kipling, have at least one paw in a symbolic (or worse, allegorical) world; Grahame's beasts are of flesh, fur and blood, and their human qualities mysteriously do not diminish, but enhance, their animal natures.

As I've already said, with every rereading *The Wind in the Willows* lends texture and meaning to my experience of life; with each familiar unfolding of its story, I experience a new happiness. This is because *The Wind in the Willows* is a magical book. Something in its pages re-enchants the world, makes it once again wonderfully mysterious. I envy the reader who is about to begin it now, who has yet to enter its welcoming landscape and who has yet to meet the comrades of a lifetime.

ALBERTO MANGUEL is a reader who lapses from time to time into writing, and who, a few years away from the prescribed three score and ten, now spends most of his time rereading. Among his favourite books are *Alice in Wonderland*, *The Adventures of Pinocchio*, *The Divine Comedy* and, of course, *The Wind in the Willows*.

The illustrations in this article by E. H. Shepard appeared in an edition published in 1931.

# *A Child in Africa*

ANNABEL WALKER

Most people have some memories of early childhood that remain vividly with them through life. Sometimes they are impossible to describe, being chiefly a quite indefinable feeling prompted by opening a particular book, or an atmosphere conjured by hearing a certain piece of music. Others are more easily converted into words: the details of a flower found in a lawn, the pattern on a hall floor, the smell of a great-aunt's sitting-room.

As I find such things come more readily to mind now that I'm several decades away from them, I imagine that a similar time lapse might partly explain the extraordinary freshness of *The Flame Trees of Thika*, which Elspeth Huxley wrote in the 1950s about her life in Kenya in 1913–14. That is only a partial explanation, of course: the author also happens to have a gift for conveying the experiences of a curious child. She can recreate her younger self's intense interest in details that pass others by: her minute observations of and passionate attachments to creatures of various kinds; her acceptance of circumstances that only age and experience judge bizarre or eccentric. And she is a talented storyteller. With a light touch and expert comic timing, she not only recreates a time and a place but also subtly develops the story of the adults closest to her, so that the end of her pre-war life at Thika brings a conclusion of another sort as well.

Elspeth Huxley's parents belonged to that class of people who saw in East Africa an opportunity to do better than they had managed elsewhere. Her gentle, optimistic father – known as Robin in the book though his real name was Josceline Grant – had 'unfortunately' been left some money when young and had made a habit of going into partnership with men who were full of good ideas but short on capital: 'By a series of extraordinary mischances, something invariably went wrong, and it was always Robin's little bit of cash that vanished, together with the partner.' After the final 'mischance', known amongst them as 'The Crash', the family arrived in Nairobi in search not only of sunshine, sport and independence but also 'the rebuilding of lost fortunes'.

What they found were 500 acres of grass and bush, sold to Robin as the 'best coffee land in the country' on a 99-year lease by Roger Stilbeck, a splendid rogue wearing an Old Etonian tie and a perfectly cut suit. Notwithstanding Robin's vision of a stone house approached by an avenue and surrounded by orchards and plantations, they remained for fifteen years in the thatched hut that had been built immediately they arrived as a temporary measure. On the beaten earth floor and against the reed-lined walls their few salvaged possessions looked incongruous in the extreme: an elegant French bureau, 'a fat-bellied commode' and some fine china coffee cups that, unsurprisingly, 'dwindled rapidly in number'.

The contrasts between the values of the white incomers and those of the local people were baffling to many on either side of the cultural chasm and rich with comic possibility, which Huxley exploits with affectionate wit. The 6-year-old Elspeth, on the other hand, was almost as much a stranger to British social conventions as to those of the Kikuyu, and approached every encounter with equal interest. Her preferences, however, are clear: given the choice, she would far rather look for buffalo in the forest with a member of the elusive Dorobo tribe, for example, than conform to the bourgeois formalities of life in the house of her prim Scottish neighbour, Mrs Nimmo.

Mrs Nimmo and the Dorobo tribesman – who, incidentally, inhabited such utterly different worlds that little Elspeth was perhaps the only thing they had in common – are only two in a cavalcade of characters that dances through the book. Whether native farm workers or British Army officers, whether major players in the story or only briefly mentioned, they all leap from the page in the brilliant spotlight of Huxley's prose. Here, for example, is the manservant Ahmed:

> a tall, thin, proud Somali who wore a shawl of bright tomato-red wound loosely round his head, and who appeared to disdain all that he saw. To him, no doubt, we were fat, effete, root-bound heathen southerners who consorted with dogs and ate pork; only loyalty, the virtue next to courage, obliged him to come amongst us, like an eagle in a parrot cage.

Elspeth, being so young, has no preconceptions, merely an infectious curiosity about everything and everyone she encounters. She notices that when a neighbour laughs, 'his teeth behaved as if they led a separate life and were saying something on their own'; the cook's ghoulish (and untrue) warnings about the Kikuyu people only make her regard them 'with a new interest'; and she loves the 'hot, jungly smell, as thick as treacle', of a tent in daytime. She has particularly enjoyable encounters with lizards, the 'nicest' visitors in the house, with Twinkle, her pet duiker (a small antelope), and Moyale, a pony given to her as a present. Even-handedly she also describes the habits of red ticks and jiggers, the latter a sand flea that lays its eggs under one's toenails. 'It was the female who caused all the trouble,' she observes. 'Male jiggas [*sic*] either leapt about at large, or displayed the masculine habit of clustering together, in this case round the eyes or ears of dogs and chickens, evidently the clubs, lodges and messes of the jigga world.'

Elspeth was fortunate in her parents. Her father seems to have had a sunny disposition and her mother was evidently a woman of immense character, resourceful, positive and practical. They also appear to have shared a well-developed sense of humour: perhaps that was what kept them together through numerous turns of fate. Elspeth's mother 'Tilly', as she is called in the book – in fact Nellie Grosvenor, daughter of an impecunious branch of that family – deals calmly with most things that life in Africa throws at her, including murderous fights between servants, an absence of amenities of any sort at her new home and an extremely limited social circle. *En route* to their land for the first time through 'roadless country', Robin wonders how the carts bearing their belongings will reach their property, since there are no bridges. '"Then we must get some built," Tilly replied. She never dwelt for long on difficulties.'

Diane Mallwick

The reader senses that Elspeth developed a similarly cheery resilience early in life. Her experiences in Kenya included adventures with pythons, the loss of Twinkle and parting from her beloved Moyale, not to mention deaths, diseases, an unaccompanied overnight train journey and seeing her father go off in search of his old regiment at the outbreak of the First World War. Perhaps the most arresting moment in her story comes when she hears of the death of a friend of her mother's, with whom she has recently stayed. Realizing that this death was the culmination of a sequence of events begun by her meeting the Dorobo, she resolves to put her faith in 'the deepest magic of the Kikuyu' to protect herself from the terrifying thought that 'some force beyond all comprehension moved one about like a counter on a board'.

Throughout *The Flame Trees of Thika* runs the thread of another tale, that of the Palmers who come to live nearby. The delectable

Lettice and her cardboard cut-out military husband bring with them a hint of mystery, since their reasons for being in a place to which they seem so unsuited are unclear. Elspeth is deeply impressed by Lettice, whose 'skin was so thin that you could see the veins under it, like a leaf in spring', and hypnotized by her friend Ian Crawfurd, whose face 'drew your eyes because its expression was always changing, like cloud-shadows on mountains, and because the bones were so beautifully formed'. Lettice's husband, Captain Palmer, meanwhile, provides an entertaining foil for Elspeth's family: a fair, handsome man with a 'vigorous moustache' who 'stood as stiffly upright as one of the posts, surveying the scene with an air of male superiority and contempt for women's prattling, combined with a touch of pasha-like complacency'.

What became of the Palmers ultimately Huxley does not relate. But the Captain's inflexible, uncomprehending approach to employing 'natives', besides being a source of amusement, only serves to highlight her own parents' generous, tolerant and humane regime, at a time when white people assumed the right to appropriate land in Africa and employ its occupants for their own purposes. Those who like to make political judgements about books with the benefit of hindsight may find this book wanting – but the rest of us can enjoy it for its charm, sympathy, spirit and wit, and for the glimpse it provides of an extraordinary fragment of history.

ANNABEL WALKER grew up in the tamer – but no less fascinating – environment of Dartmoor, where she still lives.

# *Desert Wisdom*

JUSTIN MAROZZI

I first came across Ahmed Hassanein Bey when bumping across the Libyan Sahara by camel with a friend. This was long before Kindles and iPads helped the bibliophile traveller lighten his load. Between us we had a slightly hodgepodge library consisting of a Koran, a New Testament (a Christmas present from my mother, inscribed with Deuteronomy 2:7: 'The Lord your God has blessed you in all the work of your hands. He has watched over your journey through this vast desert'), some Oscar Wilde short stories, P. G. Wodehouse, Trollope, the complete works of Shakespeare, a volume of poetry, Homer's *Odyssey* and an Arabic language book. Lawrence's *Seven Pillars of Wisdom* and Hassanein Bey's *The Lost Oases* completed the collection to be borne across the desert by our diminutive caravan of five camels: Asfar, Gobber, The Big White, Bobbles and Lebead.

Thank goodness for *The Lost Oases*. It tells the story of a truly epic journey of 2,200 miles by camel from the tiny Egyptian port of Sollum on the shores of the Mediterranean to Al Obeid in what was, in 1923, Anglo-Egyptian Sudan. As leader of this remarkable seven-month expedition, which discovered the 'lost' oases of Jebel Arkenu and Jebel Ouenat, Hassanein Bey was awarded the Founder's Medal by the Royal Geographical Society in 1924. The director of the Desert Survey of Egypt hailed it as 'an almost unique achievement in the annals of geographic exploration'.

Hassanein Bey is the perfect guide to the Sahara, whether for an

---

Ahmed Hassanein Bey, *The Lost Oases* (1925)
Long Riders' Guild Press · Pb · 520pp · £14.99 · ISBN 9781590481462

armchair enthusiast or desert traveller. Born in 1899, he was the son of the Sheikh of Al-Azhar, Egypt's equivalent of the Archbishop of Canterbury, and grandson of the last Admiral of the Egyptian fleet. Educated at the University of Cairo and at Oxford, where he won a fencing Blue, he served as Arab Secretary to the British Commanding Officer in Cairo during the First World War. Later he became an adviser to King Fuad and tutor to Prince Farouk. He also represented Egypt at fencing in the Olympics of 1920 and 1924.

Ahmed Hassanein Bey: the perfect guide to the Sahara

Good as T. E. Lawrence undoubtedly is – and he takes some beating as a writer on the desert – Hassanein Bey brings an extra quality to his literary travels. He may be a hugely urbane (and urban) sophisticate, but he is no infidel outsider. He does not need to be an accomplished Arabist or Orientalist because he speaks Arabic as an Arab, and he shares the faith, albeit less fatalistically, of those among whom he travels. Perhaps more important than any of this for *Slightly Foxed* readers, he writes like a dream.

As he sets off he ponders the allure of the desert. 'It is as though a man were deeply in love with a very fascinating but cruel woman. She treats him badly, and the world crumples in his hand; at night she smiles on him and the whole world is a paradise.' He is completely smitten.

Like all good explorers, he ignores advice from the doomsayers. A rich merchant from the Zawya tribe warns him not to travel south from Kufra:

> This journey you propose to make is through territory where no Beduin has passed before. The *daffa* [waterless trek] between Ouenat and Erdi is a long and hazardous one. God be merciful

> to the caravan in such heat. Your camels will drop like birds before the hot south winds.

Some of his camels do drop, a loss which affects him keenly. Hassanein Bey is a humane explorer whose guidelines for desert travel remain essential reading almost a century after he wrote them. Before I left for Libya, I consulted a Royal Geographical Society publication on desert navigation. *The Lost Oases* was the literary supplement.

'Nothing is more important in trekking than the condition of your camels,' Hassanein Bey writes. 'Not only must they be fat and well nourished at the start, but they must be allowed to drink their fill with deliberation and permitted to rest after the drinking.' Leaving the Libyan oasis of Jalo, he remarks that a sense of humour is 'almost if not quite the most valuable asset in desert travel'. It's an asset he certainly possesses. Whoever described the stomach-tightening cravings that assail the plodding desert traveller more amusingly than Hassanein Bey? Approaching Kufra, his mind wanders to elusive delicacies.

> As I stride along I imagine myself in Shepheard's Grill Room in Cairo and I order Crevettes à l'Americaine with that subtle variation of Riz à l'Orientale which is a speciality of the house. Or I am at Prunier's in Paris ordering Marennes Vertes d'Ostende, followed by a steak and soufflé. Perhaps it is the Cova at Milan and a succulent dish of Risotto alla Milanese; maybe Strawberries Melba at the Ritz in London . . .

His reverie is rudely interrupted by a man passing him a handful of wizened dates.

Sometimes Christian travellers in Muslim lands get the wrong end of the stick when it comes to religion. This was particularly true in the nineteenth century, when British travellers like James Richardson, a Christian campaigner against the slave trade, dismissed much Islamic practice as blind superstition. Hassanein Bey does not fall into this trap. Although ordinarily he inhabits a world very far removed from that of the uneducated desert tribesmen, he shows a deep empathy with their religious rituals.

> In the desert, prayers are no mere blind obedience to religious dogma, but an instinctive expression of one's inmost self. The prayers at night bring serenity and peace. At dawn, when new life has suddenly taken possession of the body, one eagerly turns to the Creator to offer humble homage for all the beauty of the world and of life, and to seek guidance for the coming day. One prays then, not because one ought, but because one must.

Our small caravan broke up once after a serious disagreement with our septuagenarian Tubbu guide, a descendant of the troglodyte Ethiopians praised by Herodotus as being 'by far the swiftest of foot' of any nation. We should have listened more carefully to Hassanein Bey, who explained the strict hierarchy of the desert caravan.

> It is the etiquette of the desert that no one may interfere with the guide in any way. The guide of a caravan is exactly like the captain of a ship. He is absolute master of the caravan so far as direction is concerned, and must also be consulted as to the starting and halting times.

These days, with the profoundly unromantic accessories of sat-phones and GPS devices, the desert traveller is unlikely to be dicing with death. When Hassanein Bey undertook his journey, it was a distinct possibility. He caught the tribesmen's approach to the ultimate adversity wonderfully well in the following passage:

> The desert can be beautiful and kindly, and the caravan fresh and cheerful, but it can also be cruel and overwhelming, and the wretched caravan, beaten down by misfortune, staggers desperately along. It is when your camels droop their heads from

thirst and exhaustion – when your water supply has run short and there is no sign of the next well – when your men are listless and without hope – when the map you carry is a blank, because the desert is uncharted – when your guide, asked about the route, answers with a shrug of the shoulders that God knows best . . . it is then that the Beduin feels the need of a Power bigger even than that ruthless desert. It is then that the Beduin, when he has offered his prayers to this Almighty Power for deliverance, when he has offered up his prayers and they have not been granted, it is then that he draws his jerd around him, and sinking down upon the sands awaits with astounding equanimity the decreed death. This is the faith in which the journey across the desert must be made.

The highlight of Hassanein Bey's astonishing journey was the discovery at Ouenat of 10,000-year-old cave paintings of lions, giraffes, ostriches, cows and gazelles created at a time when the Sahara was covered with wetlands. In one cave there were pictures of people swimming, a discovery later made famous by the film of *The English Patient*. This expedition was Hassanein Bey's last as an explorer. His political career continued apace until 1946, when he was tragically killed in a car accident.

Every page of *The Lost Oases* carries the unchecked passion for the desert of this most romantic, erudite and humane of writers, who perhaps better than anyone captures the paradox of this haunting wasteland: 'The desert is terrible and merciless, but to the desert all those who once have known it must return.'

JUSTIN MAROZZI is the author of *South from Barbary: Along the Slave Routes of the Libyan Sahara*. He is writing a history of Baghdad but would rather be back in the desert.

# *I'll Be Gloria*

LAURENCE SCOTT

The big news of 1966 was that Horace McCoy's classic American crime thriller *They Shoot Horses, Don't They?* was no longer my number one true love. It was Shelagh Spaul.

Shelagh was 16, and so was I. London was swinging and the sexual revolution was in full flight. Most weekdays I would cycle to Shelagh's house from my school in north London, in the forlorn hope of revolutionary activity. On this occasion, however, when I arrived in the pouring rain, it was her uncle Sidney who opened the door.

'Shelagh's not back from school yet,' he said, in a voice so parodically camp it might have come from *Round the Horne*.

I'd heard about Uncle Sidney, though we'd never actually met. I'd heard that he'd just reached the half-century, that he lived in Shelagh's family home, and that he worked nights in a sorting office.

I stood in the porch dripping puddles; he stood in the doorway wearing fluffy pink mules, a peaked cap with 'Royal Mail' on the front, and an almost transparent black silk kimono. I could tell he was naked under there, that his skin had probably never seen the sun, and that he shaved where I was sure most men didn't.

Desperate not to upset the relative of the only female on earth prepared to feign interest while I spouted memorized dialogue from my favourite fiction, I thought it a good idea to disguise my dropped jaw and bulging eyes by staring at something. Unfortunately, the something I stared at was Uncle Sidney's groin.

---

Horace McCoy, *They Shoot Horses, Don't They?* (1935)
Serpent's Tail · Pb · 128pp · £7.99 · ISBN 9781846687396

'Come and wait in my room,' he said. 'You can rub yourself off with a towel.'

The layered complexity of this invitation went straight through my adolescent brain. In fact, almost everything went straight through my adolescent brain. Despite efforts to the contrary, the only things that stayed in there were facts about cars, three notes of a blues harmonica riff, and just about every word of dialogue in McCoy's novel.

*They Shoot Horses, Don't They?* is about two young unemployed Hollywood film extras. Gloria, whose early life was full of abuse and hardship, has a protective shell of despairing wit; while Robert, raised on a farm, is a gentle, sincere man who longs for open skies and a chance to direct films. Trying to survive the Great Depression – there were an estimated 20,000 unemployed film extras in Hollywood at the time – they decide to enter a marathon dance competition because you get 'free food, and free bed as long as you last and a thousand dollars if you win'.

The story begins in a court of law where Robert is about to be sentenced to death for killing Gloria. The narrative is Robert's first-person retelling of the events that led to the killing, and his attempt to convince us that ending Gloria's life was an act of friendship, not brutality.

Uncle Sidney's room was on the lower ground floor. The curtains were closed, and there was a dim table lamp draped in a lace shawl. He shut the door behind us.

'Take your blazer off and put it by the Belling,' he said.

I put it by the Belling. Steam rose instantly.

'There's something of the beast about damp wool,' he said, handing me a towel.

There were paperbacks everywhere – on the floor, on the shelves, on the bed. Hammett, Chandler, Cain, McCoy . . . I dried my hair as Uncle Sidney's voice morphed into an American Bacall-Bogart hybrid.

'Let's go sit and hate a few people,' he said.

I recognized the phrase immediately. It comes from *They Shoot Horses*, and it's spoken by the doomed Gloria.

I quickly replied with a few words from Robert. 'I know what you mean,' I said, in my best American 'noir'. 'I know exactly what you mean.'

'You can be Robert,' said Uncle Sidney. 'I'll be Gloria.'

That was okay with me, I role-played all the time. Not only Gloria and Robert, for whom I had a soft spot, but also Rocky Gravo, the dance marathon's cynical, manipulative MC, whose personality I loathed but revelled in. I'd cycle past queues at bus stops shouting his catch phrase, 'Give, people. Give.'

Sooner or later we all seem to come across a novel that fools us into thinking great writing is easy and 'world-renowned novelist' a realistic job option. McCoy's simple, pared-down prose did it for me.

McCoy's 'simple' prose, in fact, took him years to master. He developed his craft working as a journalist and writing short stories for the now legendary magazines *Black Mask* and *Detective Dragnet*. His first novel, *They Shoot Horses, Don't They?*, published in 1935, was followed by three others, *No Pockets in a Shroud*, *I Should Have Stayed Home*, *Kiss Tomorrow Goodbye*, and numerous film scripts, including uncredited work on *King Kong*.

I was never any good at dancing, but when Uncle Sidney rested his hands on my shoulders and began to shuffle around the edges of his Turkish rug, it was easy to join in.

'Some of the girls think it will take 2,000 hours to win,' he said, in his Gloria voice.

'I hope not,' I said in my Robert voice. 'I don't believe I can hold on that long.'

Uncle Sidney removed his hand from my shoulder, and placed it on my waist. After each lap of the rug he would slump slightly, resting more and more of his weight on me, as if hundreds of marathon hours were passing. 'I'm going to get off this merry-go-round,' he said in his Gloria voice. 'I'm through with the whole stinking thing.'

'What thing?' I said, in my Robert voice.

'Life,' he said, in his Gloria voice.

In the novel, Gloria, exploited by Gravo and the event promoter Socks Donald, talks increasingly of suicide as McCoy moves his themes toward the climax that so impressed French existentialists back in the 1940s and '50s. Camus, Sartre and Malraux all sang McCoy's praises. Simone de Beauvoir called the book 'the first existentialist novel to have appeared in America'. It's never been out of print.

Uncle Sidney stepped back and let his kimono fall to the floor. Except for his Royal Mail cap and fluffy pink mules, he was stark naked – my first ever view of an unclothed, completely un-haired, mature male. I noticed that his chalk-white skin was pink in places. Places I'd rather not have noticed.

'Go ahead,' he said, in his Gloria voice. 'You know the only way to get me out of my misery.'

I hasten to add that, while Sidney's words were from the novel, his nakedness was a contribution all of his own. It's the novel's penultimate scene, the one where Gloria, realizing that callous brutality and perpetual endurance *are* her life, takes a gun from her purse, hands it to Robert, and asks him to shoot her dead. Which he does.

Totally oblivious of Sidney's libidinous intentions, overly convinced by his role-playing abilities, I could think only one thing: Sidney was about to bring out a gun and ask me to shoot him dead.

Even for someone with my limitations, it was a role-play too far.

'You'll have to do this next bit yourself,' I said.

'Do it myself?'

'Yes,' I said. 'You see, if I do it, it will be murder.'

For a few seconds the world stood still.

Eventually, Sidney lifted his cap and scratched his head, the upward movement of his arm mirrored by a lowering movement further down.

Sidney was beginning to process the possibility that somewhere along the line he had got this all wrong. I, on the other hand, was absolutely certain that I had just saved myself from a murder rap.

Late that afternoon, when Shelagh and I were alone in her room, I explained, in complex socio-political terms, that the revolution should progress with some urgency as my mother would be expecting me home for an evening meal. Shelagh then revealed her true love to be Malcolm Hicks – a boy in the year above me, whose simian gait and matching embouchure couldn't disguise the fact that he played harmonica like Larry Adler's baby brother.

A knock on the door. It was Sidney, looking smart in his Royal Mail jacket and matching trousers, peaked cap square over his forehead. He walked in and walked out again, leaving behind a tray of tea, digestives and a pencilled note with my name on it. He'd written, 'Please, don't go sit and hate me. So sorry, Sidney.'

My first true love came to an end; Shelagh and I lost touch. The last time I saw Sidney was probably the first time I understood him.

It was at Leicester Square tube station sometime in the 1970s, just a few years after homosexuality had been decriminalized in England and Wales. I was on the down escalator, Sidney was on the up. I waved. He gave a beaming smile and waved back. In his hand he held another – it belonged to a comfortable round bear of a man with a full grey beard, a cable-knit cardigan and a smile even wider than Sidney's.

McCoy, it turns out, liked to role-play too – the part of a wealthy socialite. Although he enjoyed considerable financial reward during his lifetime, it was insufficient to keep up with his outgoings. He died in Beverly Hills of heart problems in 1955, aged 58. His widow had to sell his jazz record collection to pay for his funeral.

LAURENCE SCOTT lives and writes in south-west Scotland.

# *Of Love and Lentils*

ROBIN BLAKE

Alone among the ancient classical verse forms the elegy endures as a modern one. In Augustan Rome – the world of Caesar and Cicero, but also of the elegists Catullus, Propertius and Ovid – the public uses of poetry included epic history, theology, scientific reports and political theory. To write such things in verse now would look clownish, but the spirit of Roman elegy lives on and is, indeed, at the heart of what we call poetry.

Against the tenor of very confident times, the elegists of the first century BC were wry, satirical, funny, but also doubtful, depressed and conflicted. 'I love, and I hate', Catullus wrote of Lesbia, the woman who obsessed him. Catullus, like his fellow elegists, was fascinated by the chastened reflections and secret desires of his own mind, the paradox and irony of self-knowledge, the operation of memory, the dread of loss. The modernity of his work lies not in its strict 'elegiac' metre, but in its self-examination and tone: erotic, lyrical, scabrous, black; sick with love, laughing at fate, longing for home, trembling at death. This makes the poems so adaptable to translation that they closely resemble the poetry of our own times.

All this is by way of introducing Quintilius, a rather less renowned and much later Roman elegist, whose work I first discovered in the 1970s in versions by the poet Peter Russell. They seemed an intriguing link between modernism and the Augustan sensibility; but also, from

---

The third edition of Peter Russell's *The Elegies of Quintilius* (Anvil Press, 1996) is out of print.

a personal point of view, to one puzzled by love and by the whereabouts of happiness, sharply piquant. His full name is Cittinus Aurelianus Quintilius Stultus (the last meaning 'fool') and he was born, we are told, the son of a freed Berber slave in the North African town of Sfax, in (modern) Tunisia. This was in AD 390, when the empire had long been declining into, as Edward Gibbon put it, a 'frail and mouldering edifice', corroded by luxury and deceit, and beset at almost every frontier by barbarian incursions.

It is impossible to know how such a man became a cultivated Latin author, though he hints in one poem that his father made money 'before the drachma crashed'. For the little that can be gleaned of Quintilius's early life we are entirely dependent on the few extant elegies, three of which were published in English versions by Peter Russell in 1954, and republished, with another three added, in 1975. A third edition, with extensive editorial information and another three poems attributed to Quintilius, came out in 1996.

The first elegy finds the poet living in the house where he grew up but, like Catullus and Propertius before him, depressed, out of sorts and worrying about his sex life. He looks back at the carefree interlude that has just come to an end, the time he spent with his sexy girlfriend Daunia. The two of them, he says, would haunt the gladiatorial arena, then return home in the evening for long bouts of love-making until 'dawn/Made weak the once-upright flame at our bedside'. Now, because he never got around to marrying her, Daunia has absconded with 'a rotten scum of a fellow from Rome'.

The second elegy announces a change. Unable to bear the flyblown heat of Africa and the uncouth insolence of the Vandals who roam the forum, Quintilius sells up. He crosses the Mediterranean and settles at Cagnes (in Provence) where some vestige of the old *pax Romana* can still be found. The third elegy, entitled 'The Golden Age', is the longest of the six. The poet remains disgruntled at his situation: his figs will not ripen; the book he reads is replete with an incompetent copyist's corruptions; the world beyond his door has grown so disgraceful that 'Where once sang ancient bards, base slaves are rising to cushy jobs'; and his own devotion to honour has made him 'more enemies than there are bum-boys in Sybaris'.

Given to bouts of whore-mongering and drinking (and fierce hangovers), Quintilius finds life is out of kilter. He longs (with a nod to Virgil) for 'the ancient rule of pastoral life' but knows it can never come again; his belief in the gods wavers and he has acquired a wife who secretly subscribes to the new '"Only One God" palaver' which has been spreading like a forest fire. In response Quintilius proclaims his own conversion to Christianity and his intention, which his friends think hilarious, of sailing to the Holy Land where he will live as a contemplative monk.

We next hear of him 'on the point of death' from an illness that tradition attributes (as the editor tells us) to a surfeit of lentils. Rather in the style of the famous lines ascribed to the dying Emperor Hadrian, the elegy addresses the poet's own departing soul:

> Soul of mine, do not hide in Hiemp's dismal caves, –
> Come back! Do not desert, poor wandering soul, your exiled master.

The poet longs to return to life – and to the old, full life of sensual enjoyment. From this it would appear that, if Quintilius ever did make that pilgrimage to Judea, he regretted it. At all events, his prayer is partially granted, for he does not die from the lentils and at some later date (the chronology of the six elegies is impossible to establish precisely) we find him in Liguria, still in reduced circumstances. A brief, delirious interlude of glut is granted him when he receives a gift-hamper from charitable friends in Gaul. This unleashes an outburst of poetry in praise of eating and drinking, whose composition gives his servants the opportunity to pilfer their share of the food.

After this, or perhaps at the same time, Quintilius begins to be troubled with mental illness, for there are two additional elegies appended to the canonical six, subtitled 'poems of his madness'. In the first he believes he is a badger ('I am wily, I have three back doors/ For borrowed wives and other emergencies)' while the second contains lines that indicate an almost surreal dislocation of the mind, including the delusion that 'the Wolves have taken my butterscotch'.

So, a dedicated and sensitive poet, a literary scholar, a man at odds with his times, a sensualist and gourmet, a would-be contemplative, a restless, dyspeptic, disappointed fellow and finally a lunatic: this is the complex sum of Quintilius Stultus, the poet, all packed into a mere eight short poems. It is cracking material, you would think, for a module in a university classics degree – except that you won't find one, not anywhere. A. E. Housman, classics professor and himself no mean elegist, wrote of one of the characters addressed in a poem by Ovid, 'Who was Ibis? Nobody. He is much too good to be true.' Well, Quintilius is also much too good to be true. To put that another way, he is Peter Russell's invention.

Russell was too good *not* to be true. Born in Bristol in 1921, he lived the life of an impeccable twentieth-century bohemian poet: ever impecunious, consistently accident-prone and – in the words of an obituarist – 'an accomplished and devoted drinker, and tender and appreciative womanizer'. Although he was never famous, his literary credentials were gilt-edged. After war service he ran a bookshop in Tunbridge Wells, and an avant-garde literary magazine called *NINE*, which not only introduced Quintilius to the British reader, but also Osip Mandelstam, Boris Pasternak and J.-L. Borges.

Having, almost inevitably, gone bankrupt, Russell wandered the earth for a while, living in Germany, Yugoslavia, North America and Iran, before settling in Tuscany, where he enjoyed a vivid local reputation for learning and eccentricity, until his death in 2003. His work is wide-ranging, though haphazardly published; it includes epigrams, lyrics, sonnets, translations and lengthy philosophical poems, but among the best are the poems purportedly by Quintilius, which he began to write in the late 1940s.

The *Elegies of Quintilius* might be dismissed as exercises in pastiche, except that they are too richly imagined, and too fully inhabited by their fictional author. Quintilius is a rounded persona, but his essence is his doubleness: he evokes not only the Roman world but also the late 1940s and 1950s in Britain, which are viewed with a more jaundiced eye.

> I may be a drivelling fool, a dreamer of giddy dreams
> But I know there's enough on earth for everyone to eat
> To drink, and be merry and love: that you can't carve it up
> And give out equal portions to each regardless of kind.
> That would work worse even than the present fiasco.

But there is more to Quintilius than a useful mask behind which Russell could snipe at the Attlee government and post-war austerity in general. He is also a homage to the great, mad Panjandrum of literary modernism, Ezra Pound, who had himself produced twelve elegies in the voice of Sextus Propertius. Although versions of actual Propertian poems, these wore much the same Janus-face as those of Quintilius, exploring comparisons between what Pound called the 'infinite and ineffable imbecility' of the Roman and the British Empires. Russell devoutly admired Pound. At the time when he began writing as Quintilius he was also campaigning for the release of the American poet from 'the bughouse', where he had been detained after his pro-Fascist Italian activities during the war.

Russell's identification with the old Vorticist is strongly suggested in a sketch by Wyndham Lewis, which makes Russell look like a replica of Pound at a similar age. Additionally, his Provençal home was in a region Pound loved, and his view of society is discernibly of the right, a politics that Pound much more hysterically espoused. I am happy to say, however, that the American poet's most corrosive trait, his violent anti-Semitism, is entirely absent from the Quintilius elegies. This poet is not rabidly right-wing, but benignly, even naïvely, conservative, yearning for the return of civilized order.

The last complication I must mention is the scholarly apparatus that, increasingly with each edition, accrued to the text. This links Peter Russell's Quintilius with certain early heroes of postmodernism such as Umberto Eco, Nabokov and, especially, Borges. As one of the first to publish Borges in English, Russell was well aware of the great Argentine's obsession with the imaginary book, the fictitious edition. With Borgesian relish Russell tells of his poet's lost works – *The Apotheosis of the Dildo*, the *Ars Vomitoria* – and of texts discovered in such unlikely places as the lining of an antique Swiss cuckoo clock and 'the winding sheet of the corpse of a sacred prostitute in the recently excavated Temple of Isis in Mestre'. His expansive notes follow up Quintilius's references and sources in barmy detail, and digress into such recondite areas as the uses of coconut oil in the late empire, and the original meaning of 'tungsten'.

Quintilius's literary life continued after the elegies, but it began to serve different purposes for his equally long-lived creator. In the 1980s and 1990s Russell began to publish fragments of an epic work called *The Apocalypse of Quintilius*, recording the poet's travels across the fifth-century world. In these he anticipates both Marco Polo and Christopher Columbus, reaching the borders of China and the coast of North America. Quintilius's life, we are told, became a tireless odyssey in search of true religion and the ideal woman. That seems to me to stray too far from the late classical Quintilius of the six elegies: the poet who hovers mischievously between antiquity and modernity, not quite sure if he is a pagan or a Christian, a restless intellectual or a disappointed sensualist – yet always a composer of 'stubborn verses', who could write of himself: 'His wisdom is small, but great is the folly of rulers.'

ROBIN BLAKE is editor of the memoirs of the eighteenth-century Lancashire coroner Titus Cragg, the first volume of which is entitled *A Dark Anatomy* (2011).

# *The Bird Man of Singapore*

RALPH HARRINGTON

Some bird books, the ones you take with you across mountains, into bogs or through jungles, are small in size, compact and easy to stuff into backpack or pocket, offering ready reference in all locations and in all weathers. C. A. Gibson-Hill's *British Sea Birds* is not of that kind. A large hardback, too cumbersome to take into the field, intended for the shelf in library or study, it is a work of education and of celebration. It was written by a man who loved birds for others who shared his passion, to enlighten and delight; and it merits the highest compliment one can pay to such a book – it makes one want to go out and see the birds for oneself, to get to know them as he did.

I found *British Sea Birds* in a second-hand bookshop in York and, enchanted by it, tried to find out something about the author, whose name was entirely unfamiliar to me. A little research uncovered something of the remarkable history of Carl Alexander Gibson-Hill. A doctor by training, a naturalist and ornithologist by passionate inclination, he spent most of his life in Singapore working as a zoologist and museum curator; but he was also an able historian, a gifted photographer and a tireless traveller and writer – a man who was, as Singapore's *Straits Times* said in an appreciation published after his death, 'outstanding in many fields'.

Gibson-Hill, who was born in Newcastle-upon-Tyne in 1911, qualified as a doctor in 1938, and immediately sought a medical post in some remote place where he could devote himself to natural history.

---

C. A. Gibson-Hill, *British Sea Birds* (1947) and *Birds of the Coast* (1949) are both out of print.

He managed to find such a position on tiny Christmas Island in the eastern Indian Ocean, and arrived there in the summer of 1939, having travelled largely overland, via Afghanistan, India and Indochina, on foot or by bullock-cart. Barred from active service in the Second World War by his acute short-sightedness, Gibson-Hill remained in the East and was in Singapore with his wife Margaret (also a doctor) when the city fell to the Japanese in February 1942. Margaret escaped and returned to Britain, but Gibson-Hill, who had been acting curator of the Raffles Museum as the Japanese closed in, was interned with other civilians in Changi Jail.

During his three and a half years of confinement Gibson-Hill wrote, lectured, organized entertainments (until the Japanese put a stop to them), ran the prison kitchen, and made plans for what he would do after the war. Among those plans was the writing of two books on British marine birds: the birds of the sea, and the birds of the coast. It was that project that he pursued, a free man once more, through the summer of 1946. (He had reached Britain following his release by travelling from Singapore to Cairo, then going on to Durban to join a whaler which took him to the South Atlantic – where he paused to study the birds of South Georgia – before finally completing his journey as medical officer on an oil tanker.)

Gibson-Hill's *British Sea Birds* appeared in 1947 (its companion, *Birds of the Coast*, followed two years later). It is a beautiful hardback book, adorned with a colour photograph of a Puffin on the cover which is repeated as a frontispiece. Its 144 pages contain what Gibson-Hill calls 'short biographies' of twenty-four sea birds that regularly breed in the British Isles. Some have biographies of their own ('The Gannet', 'The Fulmar'), others are gathered into groups ('The Scavenging Gulls', 'The Guillemots'). The author was very much a field naturalist, and accordingly *British Sea Birds* takes you where its author went, out among the birds, into their world. Gibson-Hill's birds, captured in his fresh, lucid prose and exquisite photographs, are not dead specimens, anatomized by a detached scientific gaze.

Paul Kershaw, 'Beclouded'

They fly free from every page, carrying the salt breeze and the sound of the waves with them.

*British Sea Birds* is a practical field guide, giving all necessary details of appearance and behaviour, but Gibson-Hill goes further, capturing in vivid, well-chosen details the elusive *character* of the birds: the Puffin's 'nautical roll', the 'strained, rapacious set' of the head of the Herring Gull, the 'erratic wandering course' followed by Storm Petrels across the face of the waves, 'like large-winged butterflies or small bats'. His pen-portrait of the Kittiwake, the 'smallest, most marine and most attractive' of the British gulls, is affectionate and precise:

> It has roughly the shape and colouring of a small Herring Gull, but it is softer and gentler in its lines. Sitting birds have a delicate, demure appearance that is quite lacking in the larger species. Even in repose the Herring Gull has the look of a brigand, while a nesting Kittiwake might be a well-pleased young woman, newly married.

By way of contrast, the Great Black-backed Gull has 'the aloofness and easy carriage of an individual always sure of getting its own way'. This proud and rapacious bird, Gibson-Hill writes, 'makes considerable slaughter among the sea birds round it, but it kills, not half apologetically as the smaller species seem to, but as though all its actions are covered by a divine mandate'.

The man who wrote those words had lived through the siege and capitulation of Singapore and had only lately returned to a war-battered Britain from captivity at the hands of the Japanese. Unsurprisingly, *British Sea Birds* is not free from the shadows cast by war. When Great Skuas are disturbed, Gibson-Hill writes, they respond with 'a systematic attack', swooping 'straight at one's head from a considerable height':

> There is little doubt that they aim at frightening the intruder rather than injuring him; the effect is like that of Japanese dive-bombing. One is not likely to be hit, but the difficulty lies in assuring oneself in advance that one is not going to be.

Dark memories are at work there, despite the light, deprecatory tone. And when the author writes of Cormorants that 'One only has to see them, slowly winging their way home against the red glow of a fading sun, to realize why Milton gave Satan the shape of a cormorant', it is not difficult to hear further echoes of war: a recollection, perhaps, of other dark, threatening shapes purposefully crossing the sky at dusk.

It is notable, however, that when the war is consciously evoked in *British Sea Birds* it is to suggest not trauma or fear but resilience. The setting for the book, after all, is the British coast, the natural rampart of land and sea which had kept the invader at bay through the long years of conflict. Any disruption the war had brought to the birds themselves was short-lived and insignificant: a number of Gannet colonies, Gibson-Hill remarks, 'were used for bombing practice, but the damage does not seem to have been serious'. The message is that whatever turmoil the war may have brought, it was temporary: the patterns of natural life continued regardless.

By the summer of 1947 Gibson-Hill was back in Singapore. For him, as for so many of the expatriate servants of Empire, it was Britain that was a remote and little-known land: his only real home was in a country and among a people not his own. He was a prominent figure

Kathleen Lindsley,
'Shags below Waterstein Head'

in colonial Singapore, becoming Director of the Raffles Museum in 1957; but by the early 1960s independence was approaching, and with it the loss for Gibson-Hill of career, home and social position. In addition, he feared that his already poor eyesight was deteriorating further, and that he, the indefatigable and precise observer and recorder of the world around him, was going blind. The impending loss of everything that mattered to him seems to have been too much to bear, and on 18 August 1963 he killed himself with an overdose of sleeping tablets.

RALPH HARRINGTON is a historian who has long been interested in birds. His own contribution to British bird-watching took place during a field trip on the Isle of Purbeck in 1977 when, over-stimulated by the sight of a Dartford Warbler, he wandered off into the Dorset countryside, became lost, and had to be rescued by the police.

# *Ignatius against the World*

MICHELE HANSON

I came upon John Kennedy Toole's *A Confederacy of Dunces* in the early Eighties, and was at once rather taken by its main protagonist, Ignatius J. Reilly. I had never come across such a repulsive hero.

Ignatius is 30, unemployed, slothful, hugely overweight, flatulent, conceited, dependent on, and absolutely horrid to, his maroon-haired mother, with whom he still lives in uptown New Orleans. He arrives on the first page – wham! – an enormous, colourful and disruptive creature in a bizarre outfit which he considers entirely sensible. It includes a green hunting cap with earflaps which

> stuck out on either side like turn signals indicating two directions at once . . . [and] prevented head colds. The voluminous tweed trousers were durable and permitted unusually free locomotion. Their pleats and nooks contained pockets of warm, stale air that soothed Ignatius . . . [To him] the outfit was acceptable by any theological and geometrical standards, however abstruse, and suggested a rich inner life.

We are only on page 2, but already I have grown fond of Ignatius, and I remain so throughout the book, despite his faults and his hypersensitive pyloric valve which closes at the least hint of stress and leads to chronic flatulence and bloating. Why am I not revolted by him? Because Toole writes about him so beautifully, with such a uniquely surprising turn of phrase and such great empathy. Perhaps

---

John Kennedy Toole, *A Confederacy of Dunces* (1980)
Penguin · Pb · 416pp · £8.99 · ISBN 9780241951590

this is because there is some of Toole in Ignatius. The modern world, for the most part, offends them both (Ignatius much prefers the medieval world of Boethius and lutes), they both have experience of work in a small, family-run factory and of selling food on the streets, and they both have an unusually close relationship with their mother.

Toole himself was born into a middle class family in 1937 in New Orleans. His mother seems to have been intensely involved in his affairs from an early age, egging him on to perform. By the age of 10 he was on stage as an actor and impressionist, and as a young academic in New York and then in Louisiana he continued to thrill the party circuit with his sharp and sparkling wit. When he was drafted into the army, he began to write this picaresque tale, set in New Orleans in the 1960s, returning to his parents' home to finish it when he was discharged. The title is taken from Jonathan Swift's 'Thoughts on Various Subjects, Moral and Diverting': 'When a true genius appears in the world, you may know him by this sign, that the dunces are all in confederacy against him.'

Ignatius sees himself as a genius battling the dunces, but Toole did not realize, while writing, that he too would be up against them before long. The novel was initially greeted enthusiastically by a publisher, who asked Toole to revise it, which he obediently did. But then the publisher rejected it on the grounds that it 'wasn't really about anything'. In despair Toole turned to drink and headache medication, took a trip around the country and ended up in Mississippi, where, in 1969 at the age of 32 he committed suicide in his car.

Ten years later, his book was published, thanks to the relentless efforts of his mother, who sent it to Walker Percy, a Southern writer and professor at Loyola University, New Orleans. He was stunned by its brilliance. Thank heavens for Percy and Mrs Toole! One year after its publication *A Confederacy of Dunces* won the Pulitzer Prize – which just goes to show that an author should: a) not always trust publishers' judgements; b) enlist his or her mother's help before doing anything drastic and, most important; c) never give up.

The publisher who rejected Toole's book was quite wrong. Far from being 'not really about anything' it is about nearly everything: New Orleans in the early Sixties, eccentricity, alienation, contemporary attitudes to race and gender, poverty, terror of communism, family relationships and the state of society – surely enough for anyone. It tells the story of Ignatius's attempts to find work and sort the world out, while he and his mother both try, in their own rather odd and tempestuous way, to separate.

Like Toole, Ignatius is living with his mother while writing his masterpiece, which will 'show literate men the disaster course that history had been taking for the past four centuries'. To Ignatius, 1960s New Orleans is 'a flagrant vice capital', filled with 'anti-Christs, alcoholics, sodomites, drug addicts, fetishists, onanists . . . frauds, jades, litterbugs and lesbians'.

But a financial calamity at home forces him to seek employment, and out into the French Quarter he goes, like a giant galleon into the village pond, with unshakeable faith in his own brilliance and perfection – 'the grandeur of my physique, the complexity of my world view, the decency and taste implicit in my carriage . . .' He finds, or rather bludgeons his way into, his first job at the Levy Pants factory, into which his huge bulk and ego can barely fit. Having whipped up the workforce, caused a strike and almost bankrupted the business, he moves on to work as a hot-dog vendor, though he eats most of the hot dogs himself.

Throughout these endeavours, he corresponds in a rather vicious and competitive way with Myrna Minkoff, 'a loud, offensive maiden from the Bronx' and a friend from his student days, who upsets him profoundly with her exhortations to 'do something' with his life, 'get out of that womb house' and sort out his 'psycho-sexual crisis . . . Open your heart, Ignatius,' urges Myrna, 'and you will open your valve.'

Outrageous, colourful and fabulously ghastly, Ignatius and Myrna, like all the book's characters, could be mistaken for caricatures. Yet Toole has made them too horribly, physically real for that. You can almost smell the people and the places, feel the crush and the heat, sense the bristling fear of communists, taste the vile hot dogs that Ignatius attempts to sell and rams into his own whiskery mouth.

In contrast to the factory-owner Levy's luxurious home – 'a permanently seventy-five-degree womb connected to the year-round air-conditioning unit by an umbilicus of vents and pipes that silently filled the rooms with filtered and reconstituted Gulf of Mexico breezes and exhaled the Levys' carbon dioxide and cigarette smoke and ennui' – Ignatius and his mother live in a neighbourhood that had 'degenerated from Victorian to nothing in particular, a block that had moved into the twentieth century carelessly and uncaringly – and with very limited funds . . . A frozen banana tree, brown and stricken, languished against the front of the porch, the tree preparing to collapse, as the iron fence had done long ago . . . There were no shrubs. There was no grass. And no birds sang.'

This environment would crush lesser beings, but the Reillys are survivors. Like almost all the book's protagonists, they may seem superficially frightful, but one cannot dislike them. Well I can't, because they are so brave and battle on with life, although the odds seem stacked against them. They are all a testament to the vibrancy of a lost New Orleans and their attempts to cope are almost superhuman, particularly those of Jones, a young black man, who we first come across in the police station 'eyeless behind space-age sunglasses', puffing clouds of smoke.

Jones must find a job or be arrested for vagrancy. He is offered one at the Night of Joy bar, where much of the action takes place. Jones is sharp as a tack and skilfully sums up attitudes to black people as he describes an elderly lady trying her best to avoid contact with him on the bus. 'Look at that. She think I got siphlus and TB and a hard on and I gonna cut her up with a razor and lif her purse. Ooo-wee.'

It is tremendously difficult to describe racism in a humorous, non-earnest, yet still biting way, but Toole does it with great success.

He shows us intolerance through the eyes of 'negroes', rather than whites. Jones and the black factory workers are the sensible ones here. The whites are the idiots who haven't a clue, although they are convinced of their own liberal and enlightened sensitivities. Ignatius feels 'something of a kinship with the coloured race because . . . we both exist outside the inner realm of American society'.

Meanwhile, from the bottom of the social pile, Jones bravely fights his way up, along with the rest of this cast of unfortunates, against overwhelming odds. Patrolman Mancuso doggedly attempts to catch a criminal, Mr and Mrs Levy battle with their poisonous marriage and mutual loathing, and Ignatius's mother struggles to cope with her enraging and useless son. Although worn to a frazzle, she still has tremendous spirit and fights to build herself some sort of personal life. One can only applaud them all, which makes *A Confederacy of Dunces* – though it may be something of a shock to current sensibilities – rather uplifting.

In the book there is a sudden and convenient happy ending for everyone who deserves it. Everyone that is except for John Kennedy Toole himself, because in his case, sadly, the dunces won. They deprived us of the potential works of a 'true genius' – the books that Toole would probably have written, had they not crushed him to death with their rejections. But they haven't won totally, because we still have this book. Read it and help my campaign to wreck their victory.

As well as writing *Guardian* columns, MICHELE HANSON has now broken out and written a memoir of her suburban childhood in the Fifties, *What the Grown-ups Were Doing*. She still lives with her two dogs and rather too many uninvited mice.

# *You Won't Look Back*

RICHARD CONYNGHAM

Who are they, I wonder, these elderly gentlemen fast asleep in the red leather armchairs? Retired brigadiers whiling away their autumn years in a room full of books, or eminent scholars dreaming of literary pursuits? That young woman with the windswept hair, foraging in Fiction S–Z, is she a lost and lonely bibliophile or the next Rebecca West? And how can that dandyish fellow in the crimson sports jacket afford to scoff and snort through the periodicals all day?

When the editors of *Slightly Foxed* first suggested I take my editorial work to the London Library, I confess I knew very little about the place. From afar, it seemed a refuge for posh authors and a pit-stop for peers *en route* to their clubs, not a place for an unkempt youth like me. And yet, at the *Slightly Foxed* office, the situation was becoming urgent. With the cocker spaniels growing increasingly distracting and the phones always ringing, how was the editorial assistant ever to do his work? The London Library was the obvious solution, but then there was the issue of the membership fee.

In the end, it was a customer at the *Slightly Foxed* bookshop on Gloucester Road who had the final word. Overhearing my doubts, he leant across a shelf of battered green Penguins and boomed: 'My boy, at £1.20 a day, it's a steal. You won't look back.' And so it was that two weeks later, on a frosty January morning, I set out for 14 St James's Square with a list of titles to take out on loan, a catalogue to write, and a newly acquired membership card to guard with my life.

Having twice missed its entrance, I eventually found the Library tucked away in the west corner of the square, between the Cypriot

Embassy and the East India Club. Abandoning my coat and umbrella in the Issue Hall, I bounded up the red-carpeted staircase, past the Reading Room and the portraits of the Library's former presidents, among them Tennyson, Eliot and Leslie Stephen, to the lowest floor of the Literature stacks. It was barely 10 o'clock but the narrow, book-lined passages, with their low ceilings and softly puttering fluorescent lights, gave the illusion of night. Squinting at the jacketless spines around me, I saw that I'd arrived at French fiction – Coulevain to Dumas. Some of the volumes were crisp, sturdy, yet-to-be-taken-out; others carried the marks of time: scuffed edges on brittle, ornate bindings. Wandering further, fishing out books at random, I paused in astonishment at those that were centuries older than the Library itself.

After a few minutes I realized there were two further floors above me, both partially visible through the iron-grille ceilings. With this sudden, dreamlike shift in perspective, the stacks seemed to become extended versions of themselves – towers of books rising up over three storeys. For a moment, it was as though I'd become weightless, suspended, enveloped in literature. Breathing in the scents of dust and old leather, and bewitched by the dim light and the faded russet bindings, I had fallen under the Library's spell. Much later I discovered that, from the same vantage point, Raymond Mortimer

Illustration by www.the-pen-and-ink.co.uk

had remarked: 'I feel inside the brain of mankind.' That morning I experienced a similar epiphany. Across the chasm of each passageway, it was as if the volumes were communicating silently, with me and one another.

With fifteen miles of books, a history spanning 171 years, and a seemingly endless list of distinguished past and present members, the London Library has, unsurprisingly, developed a folklore of its own. Everywhere you look you encounter the shades of the great. In idle moments I've watched Edith Sitwell stare down her nose at the staff behind the Issue Desk. On the carpeted stairway, I've passed Eliot and Forster. I've held the door to the Gents' for Dickens. In the Reading Room, I've watched a tiptoeing librarian ask the Woolfs to lower their voices. And while researching subjects for the *Slightly Foxed* catalogue, I've even rubbed shoulders with Vita Sackville-West in Topography and Darwin in Science & Miscellaneous.

Since 1841, when Goethe's *Theory of Colours* became the first of its books to be borrowed, the Library has been a remarkably generous lender. Even some of its rarest antiquarian volumes can be taken home, and 'country members' who live out of town can borrow and return theirs by post. One can only begin to imagine the unlikely corners of the world these books have visited – colonial forts, alpine cabins, farmhouses in the Outback, trading posts on the *veld* – and that's before considering the volumes whose globe-trottings preceded their acquisition, such as a collection of medical essays that, in 1790, travelled all the way to Pitcairn on HMS *Bounty*.

Yet with such literary generosity, of course, there come risks. During the Great War, for example, books were routinely dispatched from St James's Square to members at the Front. Most were returned in fine condition, but among those lost forever was one struck by a shell, together with its borrower, the poet and critic T. E. Hulme, in a trench in West Flanders. Other casualties include a selection of the Library's Conrad and Conan Doyle novels that went down with Kitchener on HMS *Hampshire* and a copy of *Mein Kampf* flung into the Atlantic by an outraged reader. The most exceptional provenance, however, must go to G. Fraser Melbourn's *The Planter's Manual: An English, Dutch, Malay and Keh Chinese Vocabulary* (1894): it sank with SS *Halcyon* off Folkestone Pier in 1916, was rescued from the depths of the Channel six months later, watermarked but intact, and donated to the London Library.

Quentin Blake

The collection is indeed a wonder, but no more so than the daily stream of readers for whom 14 St James's Square is a second home. There are some I admire, like the toiling men and women, all curiously alike in their overcoats and sensible shoes, who arrive within a minute of opening time and leave as the doors are being locked for the night. Some I loathe, like the muttering readers, the heavy breathers and the emphatic, two-fingered typists. And some I even recognize – the blonde film star whose presence draws the attention of every youth in the room, and the portly actor, familiar to me from an evening at the Cottesloe, who eyes me through a chink in his armful of books.

Initially, there were members who frustrated me with their seemingly aimless wanderings. But, over time, I grew to appreciate a rare state, exemplified by these blithe spirits, which the Library's former president Lord Annan described as 'creative laziness': that is, 'reading the books one ought not to be reading, and becoming so absorbed in them and following the trails along which they lead you, so that at the end of the day you still have most of the reading to do that you had before that morning'. This tradition, in itself a tribute to the joys of reading, is alive and well at 14 St James's Square. And, whether they know it or not, it is the likes of the elderly gentlemen dreaming in the red leather armchairs, the young Rebecca West foraging in Fiction S–Z, and the dandyish fellow scoffing over the periodicals, who are among its custodians.

Now that my year as a member has come to an end, I salute this extraordinary cast of characters and the enchanted labyrinth they inhabit. In any library, as in any book, there are many trails: long may they be followed.

RICHARD CONYNGHAM is about to cycle from Mexico to Patagonia on a shoestring. In his pannier bags he'll be carrying a Spanish phrasebook, an abridged Lonely Planet, and a handful of battered Penguins.

The London Library offers a range of membership types and payment methods. Applicants are welcome to visit the Library before joining. For more information or to arrange an introductory tour, please contact the Membership Department at membership@londonlibrary.co.uk/+44 (0)20 7766 4720, or visit the Library's website: www.londonlibrary.co.uk.

# *Potentate of the Polysyllable*

JOHN WALSH

Logorrhoeac, polymagisterial, omniglottal, panchromatic, Anthony Burgess was the most wordy literary figure I have ever met. I use those faintly ludicrous terms of praise because, before I met him, I was hardly aware of their existence. He employed them, with a thousand variants, all the time, in a dozen languages. He was the potentate of the polysyllable. To him, language was a currency: he loved to employ five-, ten- and twenty-pound words, abstruse Latinate constructions, arcane 'inkhorn terms', throwing them around like a sailor on shore leave, to show his enthusiasm for the world as he encountered it, a battlefield of huge, mostly ancient ideas which only he, like a twentieth-century Casaubon, could synthesize, using all the words in the dictionary.

Burgess disdained the ordinary, the middlebrow, the pop-cultural, the clichéd – in fact he disdained everything about dull, conformist post-war Britain whose citizens heated up their Fray Bentos steak pies and settled themselves before the television.

In the literary establishment in which I grew up he cut a faintly ridiculous figure. Among the groovy culture-vultures of the 1960s who appeared on television, he looked wrong. His saurian, goitrous, exophthalmic countenance was topped by a hairstyle that either Brilliantined his wayward locks into a Prince Valiant helmet or swept them into a luxuriant comb-over. None of the women in his life ever

---

Anthony Burgess, *Inside Mr Enderby* (1963), *Enderby Outside* (1968), *The Clockwork Testament, or Enderby's End* (1974) and *Enderby's Dark Lady, or No End of Enderby* (1984) are available in a single volume, *The Complete Enderby* (Vintage · Pb · 672pp · £10.99 · ISBN 9780099541431).

introduced him to a decent barber. His eyes were invariably crinkled from the smoke of the slim panatellas he always waved before him as he opined and pontificated in an Oxbridge-high-table delivery that concealed his suburban Manchester roots.

I first encountered his work in 1975 when I came down from Oxford. Released from the burden of reading canonical English, I could suddenly read anything. In a bookshop, on a whim, I picked up *The Doctor is Sick*, an early novel (1960) reprinted in 1973, and was entranced by its linguistic fire, the bustling comic energy with which it told the story of Edwin Spindrift, a linguistics lecturer in hospital awaiting an operation for a brain tumour. Spindrift escapes from the hospital, still in his pyjamas, and embarks on a picaresque journey through London in search of his errant wife. He falls in with gangsters and conmen, hookers and felons but never relinquishes his hold on language, the lexicon of plosives and fricatives that rule his world. The novel is clever, funny, confrontational and curiously sad about the limited power of words to articulate emotions.

From there, I moved on to *Inside Mr Enderby* (1963) and was stunned. Its combination of narrative confidence, intellectual rigour and low humour was like nothing I'd ever read. Who but Burgess would start a novel with a visit from Posterity, imagined as a seraphic schoolmarm with an unruly class of grubby scholars? The sleeping man they visit, Francis Xavier Enderby, named after the progenitor of the Jesuits, lives in Hove, the Brighton suburb where Burgess and his first wife Lynne moved into a one-bedroom furnished flat in 1960. Still single at 45, Enderby is a career poet whose study is the bathroom: he sits on the lavatory seat and composes on a makeshift table. The bath is full of drafts of poems and the remnants of his meals, both occasionally chewed by opportunistic mice.

Enderby is a messy, irritable, dyspeptic, rather disgusting man (we learn a lot about his problem with wind, the 'borborygms' and 'eructations' that issue from him along with divine afflatus). He's an unlikely fictional hero, except for two things. He is fanatical about his poetic Muse and belligerently hostile to the modern world. Constantly assailed by poetic lines and stanzas that beset him while he's making supper or walking down the street, he's also attacked by less attractive demands: from the people (invariably hostile) he meets in pubs, his landlady, the poetic charlatans who want to give him a prize. He is obsessed with the memory of his stepmother, whom he loathed but to whom he owes his livelihood (he lives off her legacy). She brings out Burgess's best comic writing:

> She had swollen finger-joints, puffy palms, wrists girdled with fat, slug-white upper arms that when naked, showed as indecent as thighs . . . Her habits were loathsome. She picked her teeth with old tram tickets, cleaned out her ears with hairclips in whose U-bend ear-wax was trapped to darken and harden, scratched her private parts through her clothes with a matchbox-rasping noise audible two rooms away . . . belched like a ship in fog, was sick on stout on Saturday nights, tromboned vigorously in the lavatory, ranted without aitches or grammar, scoffed at all books except *Old Moore's Almanac*, whose apocalyptic pictures she could follow.

There can have been few more dramatic circumstances in literary history than those which produced *Inside Mr Enderby* – provided you believe its author. The story goes like this. After years away, teaching in Malaya, Burgess collapsed in a local schoolroom in Brunei, was stretchered to a local hospital, X-rayed, examined and sent home to England, apparently with a brain tumour that would kill him in a year. Though he supplied biographers with contrasting details about this diagnosis, he swore that, with only a year to live, he resolved to write several novels that would provide his estranged, alcoholic and promiscuous wife Lynne with an income-cum-pension. Among them – five in a single year – was *Inside Mr Enderby.* He was obliged to publish it under the Kafkaesque *nom-de-plume* of Joseph Kell.

At the time of publication, Burgess was reviewing novels for the *Yorkshire Post* and the literary editor sent him a copy of *Enderby*. Assuming it was a joke, Burgess reviewed it – by no means fulsomely – and was fired when the little deception was discovered. Burgess told Anthony Clare, who interviewed him in 1988 for the radio programme *In the Psychiatrist's Chair*, that Enderby came to him in a dream:

> When I was working in Borneo in the late 1950s, I was suffering from malaria, had a slight delirium, and I went into the toilet and thought I saw a man sitting on the toilet seat writing poetry. I suppose the vision lasted a mere micro-second but the character remained, and I wrote four books about this character whom I called Enderby – very squalid, masturbatory. This I can't explain. The character has nothing to do with me, but his talent for writing poetry must be to some extent my own.

Burgess fans are not fooled. The obvious avatar is Leopold Bloom in Joyce's *Ulysses*. In the book's infamous fourth chapter, Bloom visits the outside privy at No. 7 Eccles Street, Dublin, and becomes the first character in fiction to be described in the act of purgation. While relieving himself, Bloom reads a page of *Tit-Bits* and wonders about writing a story to win a cash prize. Enderby is similarly involved in creativity and excretion.

Joyce was Burgess's hero and the subject of two of his later books, and Enderby resembles Bloom in being a squalid, furtive, dyspeptic man – but Bloom is married, with a daughter and a dead son. Enderby is solitary. He shouldn't be taken as an autobiographical portrait of Burgess, despite the Hove address. Andrew Biswell, Burgess's biographer, offers a shrewd analysis:

> [Enderby] seems in many ways to represent the roads that Burgess had not taken: if he had not married Lynne in 1942; if he had allowed his joyless childhood to develop into a full-scale

neurosis; if he had clung to his early ambition to make a reputation for himself as a poet; if he had allowed himself to grow into a less tactful, a less intelligent, a less forgiving, a less generous man than he was – then it's possible he might have come to resemble Francis Xavier Enderby. Enderby is more than merely Burgess's shadow: he is a demonic, monastic, spermatic, worst-self, a brutal auto-caricature, an anarchic anti-Anthony.

Burgess followed his anti-Anthony in three more books: *Enderby Outside* (1968), *The Clockwork Testament, or Enderby's End* (1974), which features a hilarious encounter between the poet and a new generation of ignorant American university students, and concludes with his death; and a short final volume, *Enderby's Dark Lady, or No End of Enderby* (1984), 'Composed to placate kind readers of *The Clockwork Testament*, who objected to my casually killing my hero'.

* * *

We met in 1988 when I first interviewed him in London. I was then literary editor of the *Evening Standard.* He'd just published *Any Old Iron*, his updating of the Excalibur legend. I think he realized he was dealing with a deranged fan, rather than a mere literary hack, when I broke off from enquiring about his new novel to ask: 'How was it that, in *Enderby Outside*, you wrote a sentence in which you used the word "onion" three times consecutively?'

'Ah yes,' he said. 'I remember being quite pleased with that. How did it go? "Rawcliffe lurched upon Enderby and said . . ."'

'No, no,' I interrupted. 'The sentence went, "Rawcliffe lurched across the restaurant and breathed upon Enderby, bafflingly (the restaurant refused to serve, because of the known redolence of onions, onions), onions."'

Burgess looked at me. Perhaps he wasn't used to having complete strangers reciting his work out of the blue.

'So why did you do it?'

'Oh, you know,' he said modestly, waving his panatella, 'because I could.'

I asked him about Graham Greene, his Catholic co-religionist and sometime neighbour in the south of France: Greene in Nice, Burgess in Monaco. (Though he admired the elder writer's work, Burgess had reservations about Catholic converts like Greene, finding them less sympathetic than those who, like himself, had had 'hellfire injected into their veins'.)

'Greene has a new mistress,' he said sadly, 'a married woman. Her husband has taken to walking by his apartment building most nights and shouting *salaud!* at the windows.'

We talked about a myriad other things, and at the end he posed for a photograph. I asked in my callow way if I might be included in one picture, for my study wall. We stood awkwardly together, the literary titan and his beaming new acolyte.

'Not too close,' cautioned Burgess, *sotto voce*. 'People might talk.'

* * *

In the years that followed, I noted his every appearance in the media, relishing his lordly, cigar-puffing grandeur while marvelling that he was becoming a bit of a cabaret turn. He turned up on a TV chat show called *Friday Night, Saturday Morning*, hosted by the Irish writer Frank Delaney. The first guest was the actress Sian Phillips. When Burgess settled himself upon the plush sofa, Delaney said: 'Now Anthony, you're a famous wordsmith. But can even you, who knows every word in the language, come up with any words to describe the beauty of Miss Sian Phillips here?'

Burgess regarded the woman beside him and rose to the occasion. 'Oh I think so,' he said. 'Orchidaceous. Polypulchritudinous . . .'

The studio audience clapped. You'd have thought the author of *A Clockwork Orange* and *The Malayan Trilogy* was a modern version of Professor Stanley Unwin who amused 1950s audiences with his 'gobbledegook' idiolect.

* * *

The last time we met was in February 1992, the month of his seventy-fifth birthday. I'd rung Penguin to discover what arrangements they'd made to celebrate this anniversary. None, they said. At the time, I'd been asked to set up some interviews with writers at the Brentwood Arts Centre in west London, and I seized the opportunity. Could Mr Burgess be persuaded to come over from Switzerland for an evening of discussion and Q&A in front of an audience? To my delight, he agreed.

We met backstage. Though clearly unwell – he was diagnosed with lung cancer later that year – he was in good spirits. We talked about current literary reputations. I asked if he'd seen Greene before his death the previous year.

'I regret to say we had a falling-out,' said Burgess. 'It seems that I was . . . indiscreet with a young journalist a few years ago and said something about Greene's mistress, and he sent me a letter calling me an unbalanced liar and ending our friendship.'

'But Anthony,' I cried, 'that was me! I interviewed you for the *Evening Standard* and you told me the woman's husband shouted at his windows . . .'

He regarded me coldly. I'm not surprised. My tiny footnote in literary history had meant the end of a valued, if rocky, personal relationship with someone he genuinely admired.

On stage he spoke with the old fluency about his career, his Manchester youth, his dismay that the notoriety of *A Clockwork Orange* had eclipsed his more serious works. When it was time for questions, the audience piled in.

'I finally managed to read *Ulysses* after three attempts,' said the first. 'But I can't get on with *Finnegans Wake* at all. What exactly is it about?'

'The action of *Ulysses*', Burgess replied, 'takes place in a single day. That of *Finnegans Wake* in a single night. You are dealing here in a phantasmagoria, a dreamscape, an echo-land. All thoughts and ideas and actions are conflated, and all the language is conflated too. At the centre is the family of Humphrey Chimpden Earwicker, who represents, among others, Noah . . .' and he was off on a perfectly paced mini-lecture in his best magisterial tones.

The second question concerned *À la recherche du temps perdu*. Amazingly – given the well-known *Monty Python* sketch about summarizing Proust in fifteen seconds – the questioner asked what the 3,000-page book was 'really about'. Imperturbably, Burgess explained, with many side references to Bergson's philosophy of time.

The third question was a surprise. 'Mr Burgess,' said a man in the nineteenth row, 'I know you are an accomplished cook. What is the secret of a perfect tortilla?' The audience murmured disapprovingly. This was like asking Tolstoy whether he favoured trainers or espadrilles. Burgess never wavered.

'A tortilla is no more than a potato omelette,' he replied. 'And the secret is not to fry the cubes of potato too crisply before you drench them in the ovoid mixture.' The audience cheered. 'Ovoid' indeed.

He died a year later. To think of him going was to imagine an empire crumbling. He was a serious moralist, theologian and literary bigwig in a world of ninnies and dilettantes. Meeting him was like meeting Dr Johnson, a similarly shambolic, physically uncoordinated, language-obsessed, Northern know-all. You approached him nervously, shyly asking a question like someone poking a 20p coin into a jukebox – and out would come a vast oratorio of learning and opinion. He was belligerent, argumentative and magisterial but engaging and funny too, a serious entertainer and an awesome intellectual who never forgot that borborygms and eructations were also part of the human condition.

JOHN WALSH is assistant editor of the *Independent* and can be heard on the Radio 4 literary quiz show *The Write Stuff*. His most recent book was the novel *Sunday at the Cross Bones*.

# *Artless but not Heartless*

PATRICK WELLAND

In May 1797, the 33rd Regiment of Foot Officers arrives in Calcutta. A round of parties ensues, one at Colonel Sherbrooke's 'small mansion' in the village of Alypore three miles from the city. A guest later describes the company – which includes 28-year-old Arthur Wellesley, the future Duke of Wellington – as 'eight as strong-headed fellows as could be found in Hindustan'. He recalls fondly:

> After drinking two and twenty bumpers in glasses of considerable magnitude, the considerate president said everyone might then fill according to his own discretion . . . we continued to follow the Colonel's example of drinking nothing short of bumpers until two o'clock in the morning, at which hour each person staggered to his carriage or palankeen. The next day I was incapable of leaving my bed from an excruciating headache, which I did not get rid of for eight and forty hours; indeed, a more severe debauch I never was engaged in in any part of the world.

This was praise of a high order from our guest, for 48-year-old William Hickey had behind him more than thirty years' experience of getting drunk and into trouble, be it in the bagnios and taverns of London, or in India, China or Jamaica. To call William incorrigible

---

The Folio Society edition of William Hickey, *Memoirs of a Georgian Rake* (ed. Roger Hudson, 1995), is out of print.
Fergus Linnane, *London: The Wicked City* (2003)
Robson Books • Pb • 256pp • £8.99 • ISBN 9781861059901

is vastly to overestimate his capacity for shame. He was expelled from school in 'high disgrace', became a hopeless spendthrift and was then dispatched to India by his father after embezzling his employers' funds. He was 'fixed' from his early teens in his 'attachment to women of loose and abandoned principles'. And he was a martyr to claret. He confesses: 'Society proved my bane . . . I never could flinch from the bottle . . . though always cheerful and good humoured in my cups . . . I transgressed, repented, and transgressed again, thus continuing an endless course of folly.'

Hickey today is better known as a *Daily Express* gossip column launched in 1933 by another old rogue, the future Labour MP and peer Tom Driberg. I worked at the *Express* in the early '70s and remember in my ignorance being surprised to learn that the man apparently responsible for the column had died 140 years earlier. The choice of the name, however, was apt. For William Hickey, born in Pall Mall in 1749, was a splendid observer of the English social scene at its most vibrant. And, fortunately for us, he recalls his spectacular follies and modest triumphs in his captivating *Memoirs of a Georgian Rake.*

Perhaps the best-known memoir of Georgian London is James Boswell's *London Journal, 1762–3*. Boswell, like William, is unashamed to tell us of his falls from grace. But he is armoured by his pompous self-belief and ambition for advancement. I find William more appealing, for he lacks vanity. He can never resist a daring décolletage and he is even less likely to protest at the withdrawal of a convivial cork. But he is open-hearted, generous and loyal, and acts without selfish motive. He is feckless, but not fickle. Artless, but not heartless.

William, the son of a wealthy Irish solicitor, revealed his dubious colours early on. Aged 7, he sat upon the knee of his godfather Colonel Matthews at dinner. 'Having just swallowed a bumper of claret which he had given me I, with a deep sigh, said to him "I wish I was a man." "Aye," observed the Colonel, "and pray why so, William?" To which I quickly replied, "That I might drink two bottles of wine every day."'

This precocious ambition was soon achieved. Drink is a constant feature of William's memoirs. Here he is at 13 having attached himself, while bunking school, to a river outing of the Fishmongers' Company which ended with the revellers inviting him to a turtle and venison feast at Richmond: 'I poured down champagne at a great rate . . . [and told them] I could drink as much as the best of them . . . the party sat to a late hour but I held out until they broke up, when I was so drunk that on rising from my chair I fell flat on the floor.' He did not return home until the next day. Over the following years, this prodigious appetite for the bottle led him into a succession of rumbles in which he was often more victim than perpetrator. But he always bounced back: above all, William was a happy drunk.

And then there was sex. Some of William's candid recollections were considered too ripe for publication in early editions. His childhood nanny, Nanny Harris – 'as wanton a little baggage as ever existed', he recalled with admiration – took an unseemly interest in him. Far from being emotionally scarred by what today would land Nanny in court, he continued to adore 'that infatuating jade', years later taking her as his mistress. He lost his virginity at 13 (a busy year) and by 14 was a regular habitué of brothels. Two years later, when he joined a legal partnership, it was his 'peculiar good fortune to meet with uncommonly generous and disinterested whores and rogues' and he delighted in their lusty company.

And what fun there was to be had. London in the eighteenth century was a sink of unbridled lubricity. As Fergus Linnane points out in his *London: The Wicked City*: 'There was a gusto about eighteenth-century vice unmatched before or since. The fashionable worlds of vice and entertainment were contained within a few square miles . . . more men were making more money from trade, banking, the stock market and the growing sales of luxury goods and they, or in many cases their sons, had no moral scruples about how they spent it.'

The result was a fever of gambling and a sex industry of exotic variety. In a rare display of self-discipline William forswore gambling, having been told he was so incompetent a card player he was sure to lose all. But he enthusiastically joined a riot of low life played out in pleasure gardens, drinking dens, coffee houses, bathing houses and brothels.

In his memoirs William does not explore any motive behind his relentless search for gratification. We are occasionally treated to an anguished expression of remorse and a vow to reform, but we know this is idle talk. The quest is all. However, at a time when the miserable reality of prostitution went largely unremarked, he does evince some moral scruple. He is disgusted by Wetherby's hellhole in Little Russell Street 'where such a scene was exhibiting that I involuntarily shrunk back with disgust and dismay'. Nor does he condemn or patronize. Instead, he speaks of his casual liaisons with unmistakeable affection. On one occasion he donates 10 guineas (£600 today) towards the relief of a popular prostitute, commenting: 'I had afterwards the satisfaction of hearing that this seasonable aid had probably saved the life of a deserving woman who, in her prosperity, had done a thousand generous actions.'

The mind reels at William's capacity for excess. But the reader of his memoirs will find much more than a rake's progress. William gives us an eyewitness account of the mass demonstration in support of the then imprisoned John Wilkes and its murderous suppression by troops. We meet Lord George Gordon – half-mad instigator of the bloody 1780 anti-Catholic Gordon Riots, but then 'a volatile and elegant young man of the most affable manners'. We also learn about duelling, smuggling, slavery, contemporary enthusiasms for sailing and rowing, and the eccentricities of trade and social life in India, China and the West Indies.

William made the first of three visits to India when he was sent there in 1769 after fiddling the books of his law firm to fund his dissipations. The trip was not a success and he returned to England soon afterwards via Canton. Back in London it was not long before, with his 'usual want of resolution', he yielded again to his old bad habits.

The inevitable result was more debt, more peculation, more disgrace and in 1775 a second exile, this time in Jamaica.

William returned to India in 1777 and finally achieved financial success in Calcutta as an attorney. 'Notwithstanding I lived so dissipated a life in point of drinking and late hours,' he boasts, 'no man laboured harder.' But two years later he was on his way back to London again after volunteering to bear a legal petition to Parliament. He guiltily admits: 'The idea of revisiting old haunts having once got into my giddy brain, I had neither prudence nor fortitude to resist.'

William was now 30 but he had lost none of his zest for life, and for the next four years he burned the candle with as much diligence as before. For the first time, however, he appeared genuinely to lose his heart. After chasing the courtesan Emily Warren to a disappointing finale, he fell for the delectable Charlotte Barry. The fiction of Georgette Heyer could not better the course of their amour. With considerable courage William rescued Charlotte from her jealous 'protector', the vicious Colonel Henry Mordaunt.

> Seizing a knife from the table he swore with the most horrible oaths that rather than permit her to quit his house he would bury it in her heart . . . armed with a poker I set him at defiance . . . and told him I would not stir unless Mrs Barry accompanied me. The perspiration ran down his face in streams from rage and I actually thought he must have died from passion.

The couple fled first to Lisbon and then India, enduring a hurricane on the way. Poignantly, on Christmas Day 1782, Charlotte died of a wasting fever in Calcutta, so ending the most important relationship of William's chaotic

B. Lodge

life. 'She kissed me with her almost clay-cold lips, such a kiss as I never can forget . . . safely may I say, I truly, fondly, loved her, loved her with an affection that every new day, if possible, strengthened.'

William spent the next twenty-six years in India, eventually accumulating more than 60 servants and setting up home for seven years with his Hindustani mistress Jemdanee. My edited Folio edition of the *Memoirs* devotes only 60 out of 400 pages to this period of his life. But we are left with a vivid picture of a man whose appetite for life and jovial company was undiminished. William may have achieved respectability, but, happily, the fire still burned and he spent money with abandon. In his last three years on the sub-continent he finally decided to put aside cash for his return to England and in August 1808 landed at Deal. He then settled down in Buckinghamshire before moving to London where he died in 1830.

The *Memoirs* are not reflective. William is a player, not a critic. His recollections are all the better for it. In these austere times it is a joy to read of a more vigorous world – especially in the company of such a transparently good-natured man.

PATRICK WELLAND lives in Sussex. He would love to have joined William Hickey on a night out but fears he would not have lasted the distance.

# *Iced Tea and Hospitality*

MARIE E. WICKS

At certain times in my life, I have opened a book and discovered a friend. I have chuckled with Anne Shirley over her comical escapades in the quiet town of Avonlea. I have stood under the watchful eye of Aunt Polly and scolded Tom Sawyer for skipping school, only to shrug and offer to whitewash the fence for him once her back was turned. Once I even considered inviting Jo March to dinner, though this idea was quickly dismissed, for I felt quite certain that Jo would go nowhere without her three sisters in tow and before I knew it the entire March clan would show up at my door, for which I had neither the time nor the energy. At this thought I poured myself a cup of tea, took *Little Women* down from the bookshelf, and visited Jo at her house instead.

The pleasure I gain from each visit to the March household is not unlike that feeling of elation that follows a particularly successful tree climb, or a brisk walk, or any sort of activity involving lighthearted exertion, and it could not be more different from the sense of peace rendered by the easy embrace of those who inhabit the fictional small mountain town of Mitford, North Carolina, created by Jan Karon. From the beginning, feeling at home in Mitford is as effortless as putting on a pair of well-used slippers. When we readers come

---

Jan Karon, *At Home in Mitford* (1994) and the other books in *The Mitford Years* series – *A Light in the Windows* (1995), *These High, Green Hills* (1996), *Out to Canaan* (1997), *A New Song* (1999), *A Common Life* (2001), *In This Mountain* (2002), *Shepherds Abiding* (2003), *Light from Heaven* (2005) and *In the Company of Others* (2010) – are all available as US Penguin paperbacks.

knocking, Mitford pats us on the back, invites us in, and offers us a glass of iced tea sugared with a generous dose of hospitality.

Our first encounter with the locals as we stroll through the centre of town is with Father Tim – small in stature, slightly balding, with lively eyes and a cheerful demeanour. This country parson – who will become the book's most prominent character and our eyes and ears in Mitford – is brought alive for us before we even know his name. He is the man we absent-mindedly pass by on the sidewalk as he steps out of the Main Street Grill and breathes in the honest cold of a mountain spring. We hear his thoughts before we see his face. Perhaps his unassuming manner is the reason I find it so easy to befriend Father Tim. He is far from loquacious, but his scattered musings make him a most enjoyable companion.

My entrance into Mitford begins each time, as it should, with Chapter One. As I read the first few sentences of *At Home in Mitford*, I step into the tiny town under the relaxing rays of the early morning sun. Father Tim leaves the coffee-scented warmth of the Grill and heads toward the church office. He is delighted to find himself indulging in a luxury that his schedule rarely permits: he is ambling. I close my eyes and try to remember the last time I caught myself ambling. I recall instead dashes to class across a rainy campus, jogs with my father, and my brisk pace when marching with a particular goal in mind. After a few moments of reminiscing, I open my eyes and conclude that ambling implies a lack of concern that is certainly not in my nature. Indeed, Father Tim, you are not the only one who is surprised to find yourself suddenly carefree.

For Father Tim these precious moments of leisure are short-lived, however, for as he reaches into his pocket for his key to the church office, his hand encounters something animated and cold and decidedly wet. Looking down, he meets the doleful gaze of an enormous black dog. Without a moment's hesitation, the dog rears up and places two enormous paws on Father Tim's shoulders before saluting him in canine fashion. A startled Father Tim reacts with his priestly instincts. In his sermon voice he shouts a verse from Ephesians: 'Let no corrupt communication proceed out of your mouth . . .' Before he can finish, the dog removes his paws with a sigh. This enormous creature, it seems, is controlled by Scripture.

Due to its uncanny resemblance to a particular church clerk he once knew, Father Tim names the black dog Barnabas. Barnabas, we find, is not only moved by the Word of God, he also shares Father Tim's predilection for the poetry of Wordsworth. Barnabas and Father Tim become fast friends, and it is clear that the two were meant for each other.

A shaggy, black, Romantic poet of a dog is not the only arrival to disrupt the tranquillity of Father Tim's quiet life. Enter a lovable yet unloved boy desperately in need of a home, an attractive neighbour who causes Father Tim's heart to beat unreasonably fast, and a secret that penetrates the history of the town itself, and before long the priest can only dream of finding himself with the leisure to amble.

Though I have never known a dog named Barnabas or tasted eggs and grits at the Main Street Grill, the town of Mitford is not far from the places I have truly been, the places that are home to me. During my childhood, nearly every holiday or long weekend in our family calendar was spent at my grandparents' house in Highlands, North Carolina. My grandfather believed that if Highlands did not have the same address as heaven, the two at least shared the same zip code. He would often take me, my brother and sister by the hand and bring us with him downtown. After stopping by the town visitors' centre for the latest brochures, we would wander past the cheerful shop windows and duck inside Reeve's Hardware Store, where Papa would introduce us to John the shopkeeper. Our next visit would be to the preacher of the First Baptist Church where my aunt had been married, and the pastor and Papa would smile and shake hands, and Papa would laugh in his good-natured way. No visit to town would be complete without a trip to the bank, where a bowl containing an appetizing array of lollipops would reward our ventures. At long last we would return home to the little grey house nestled among the rhododendron bushes. The screen door would give us a welcome slap as we stepped inside, greeted with a pitcher of iced tea and a cloud of savoury smells wafting from Nana's kitchen.

*At Home in Mitford* is the first in a series of novels by Jan Karon that follow the triumphs, disappointments, laughter and tears of a colourful cast of characters. No great feats of incredible daring are performed, no superhuman deeds are accomplished, and yet it is the everyday predictability of Mitford that renders it so unpredictable. When I curl up in a chair with my cup of tea on a quiet evening and tiptoe into Mitford, I am met with a down-to-earth reassurance that is more wonderful than the imagination of Tom Sawyer or the playful whimsy of Jo March. I begin to believe again in the miracles that lie hidden in the commonplace. Though my Papa passed away two years ago and any journeys to Highlands are now few and far between, I close my eyes and feel once again the firm grip of Papa's hand round mine and hear his boyish laughter as we march down Main Street licking our lollipops. The story comes to an end, my empty tea cup rests on the table, the book lies closed, and yet the memory lingers. I don't know what life has in store, what places I shall visit or what people I shall meet, but I do know that wherever I am, I will always be at home in Mitford.

MARIE E. WICKS is studying French, International Studies and Chemistry at the University of Mississippi in Oxford, Miss. A literary town, Oxford is the 'postage stamp of native soil' of William Faulkner.

# *From Harry's Bar to Delhi*

TIM MACKINTOSH-SMITH

'What *Ulysses* is to the novel between the wars and what *The Waste Land* is to poetry, *The Road to Oxiana* is to the travel book.' So says Paul Fussell in the first puff on the back cover of my thirty-year-old paperback edition of Robert Byron's 1937 masterpiece. Now, as it happens, Professor Fussell – or rather his *Abroad: British Literary Traveling between the Wars* – is sitting next to me, and what he actually said was, 'Its distinction tempts one to over-praise, but perhaps it may not be going too far to say that what *Ulysses* is to the novel . . .' etc. In the puff, the professorial hedging has been entirely clipped away. Still, it is high praise indeed. Is it deserved? That old stirrer Wilfred Thesiger thought *The Road to Oxiana*, far from being the great transformative work of twentieth-century travel, was 'a lot of nonsense'.

I don't know how many times I've travelled *The Road to Oxiana*. Probably a dozen. But one of the great things about books is that we forget them. Of course we remember if we liked a book or not, and we recall details, characters, perhaps whole chunks. From *Oxiana*, I always remember Shir Ahmad: '(*m*) Italian lady she sit beside me,' the Afghan diplomat told Byron, musing on a visit to the opera in Rome. 'She is (*eyes blazing ff*) big lady, yah! great? no, fat . . . Her breast is (*cr*) too big. (*mf*) It fall out of box, so . . . (*pp*) I am frightened. I see if it shall be in my face (*f*) I suffocate.' We remember bits and pieces like this, and general outlines. But the universe of particularities that is a book is too big for a single mind to grasp and hold.

---

Robert Byron, *The Road to Oxiana* (1937)
Penguin · Pb · 368pp · £9.99 · ISBN 9780141442099

So it is that I can set off again with Byron, heading for the blue yonder of the lands along the Oxus, but not really knowing where I'm going.

The Contents, a list of places, is a helpful memory-jog. We begin in Venice. Then we spend quite a while in Persia, then move to Afghanistan, then – hang on – we're back in Persia again; then off to Afghanistan once more. It seems we make no fewer than seven separate trips to Teheran along the way and end up, via India, in Wiltshire. Perhaps Thesiger had a point: as itineraries and narratives go, it looks nonsensical.

I'd forgotten too that there was an Introduction to my edition by Bruce Chatwin. 'Long ago,' he says, 'I raised *The Road to Oxiana* to the status of "sacred text".' Now, I respect Chatwin as a writer. I admire Thesiger. I trust the judgement of neither. So what *is* this book? Is it sacred, or is it nonsense?

And then I'm on Byron's first page, swimming at the Lido in 'water like hot saliva', drinking a cocktail of champagne and cherry brandy at Harry's Bar ('"To have the right effect," said Harry confidentially, "it must be the worst cherry brandy." It was.') and wandering round Palladio's Villa Malcontenta: 'Europe could have bid me no fonder farewell than this triumphant affirmation of the European intellect.'

From there on there's no looking back.

Once you're on the road to Oxiana, twisted though it is, you're drawn along too fast to worry about lit. crit. It's all over the place, the very opposite of the slow, single-minded Thesigerean crossing of empty quarters. The landscapes are densely peopled, heaving with characters and noise and smell and colour. Snapshots, snatches of dialogue, *objets trouvés*, realia, ephemera – letters of introduction, applications for travel permits – are pasted together with the artful abandon of découpage. Imagine a travelling trunk of Victorian times – one of those Wolseley valises, maybe, that turns into a wardrobe or a bed – grand, battered, covered in pictorial labels, and then transformed into a book – and you have some idea of what it's like.

The fact that it's all done as a diary, the entries headed with place, date and, often, altitude, gives it the verisimilitude of three-dimensional movement through time. The fact that Byron's verbs vault madly between tenses adds temporal disorientation to an already loopy route. (And this, not itineraries, is what real travel is about. Real travellers belong to a lost tribe.) It could all have gone desperately wrong, but it works brilliantly.

All this is quite apart from the topographical interest of the book. In 1933–4, Byron and his friend Christopher Sykes were travelling through an Iran and Afghanistan that happen to occupy the same spaces on the maps as their namesakes today, but were in many respects different countries. One may still be able to find the odd pipe of opium in the Islamic Republic (to Byron, smoking the poppy-wizard with a policeman, it 'tasted of potato'; perhaps he didn't inhale); one can find booze flowing freely in certain households in Teheran. But what has happened to the Iran where one could pick up a bottle of half-decent claret in a wayside caravanserai, or assault a sanctimonious cleric – as Byron did – with a bottle of arak, and get away with it? Where Christian missionaries operated freely and openly (albeit making few converts – Archdeacon Garland's score was one, during thirty years in Isfahan, and she reconverted to Islam on her deathbed)? Where any self-respecting city had British and American consulates ('"Just in time for the ball!" shouted Mrs Gastrell, as we staggered up the steps of the Consulate' – this in the Shi'ite holy of holies, Meshed)? And do Afghan soldiers march these days with roses in the muzzles of their guns?

Byron, whose best comic writing relies on bathos, revelled in the absurd juxtapositions of that lost world: *Othello* in Armenian in Teheran, say, or Sykes discussing Gibbon's *Decline and Fall* in Persian with a muleteer. Indeed, much of the territory itself was a comic misfit – between the Persia of 'the Omar Khayyám fiends' and the gimcrack-westernizing Iran of 'Marjoribanks' (Byron and Sykes's private name for the Shah). Afghanistan, he felt, was in much sounder cultural shape: 'Perhaps the Afghans have struck the mean [between tradition and westernization] for which Asia is looking.' Seen from our own much bleaker present, it all seems rich and strange.

So too does Byron himself. At first sight, he is an outrageous example of that all but extinct creature, the opinionated aesthete. 'I came to Persia', he pronounces soon after his arrival there, 'to get rid of . . . the taste of the Alhambra and the Taj Mahal.' What can one say? He only does it to annoy . . . But soon we learn to love this ranting arbiter of taste, to look forward to his poses and pontifications – and to realize how often his darts hit the mark. I'm not sure though about his attack on the unfortunate Buddhas of Bamian in Afghanistan: 'It is their negation of sense, their lack of pride in their monstrous flaccid bulk, that sickens . . .' (Perhaps the Taliban, who in 2001 destroyed the Buddhas with artillery fire – 'we turned them into dust,' they crowed, 'then we made dust of their dust' – were Byron fans.)

It's all enormous fun, but in the end it's not the point. Byron was indeed an aesthete, but he was no intellectual popinjay. All this richness and rococo grotesquerie is here as the setting for gems – cool, cut, polished, glittering – of architectural description, which I will not quote. They are what the book is really about, and they can only be read *in situ*. Reading is travel; reading Byron is also seeing – seeing buildings like the Sheikh Lutfullah mosque in Isfahan and the Gumbad-i-Kabus, that extraordinary tomb-tower, caught in eternal take-off from the Caspian steppe. Illustrations are superfluous.

So, is it sacred, as Chatwin thought? Yes, in a humanist way. The journey is mad on the map, but its sane and deeply serious intention – of looking at the material expression of human civilization – elevates it from jaunt to pilgrimage. The pilgrimage leads from Palladio's

Malcontenta and European rationalism via Islamic rationalism – Sheikh Lutfullah, the Gumbad-i-Kabus – to the beginnings of Eastern irrationalism in the 'Indian and painstaking' Qutb Minar, the huge thirteenth-century minaret of Delhi. It ends, touchingly, in England, with Byron's mother: 'What I have seen she taught me to see.'

And is it nonsense, as Thesiger said? Yes, in the sense that it explodes the norms of narrative and itinerary. Byron is the holy fool of travel writing, clothing truths about humanity and culture in a motley robe – the garb of Harlequin, the *hazarmikhi* or 'thousand-patched' cloak of the old Persian sufis.

But is it the *Ulysses*, the *Waste Land* of Travel, as Professor Fussell thought it might be, if it wasn't going too far to make the claim?

No. Many before Byron travelled the same road, even if it didn't lead to Oxiana. Byron's inscribed copy of Norman Douglas's *Old Calabria* represented, he told the older author, 'the imprint of one mind upon another'. That imprint is clear to see. Byron follows, so to speak, in Douglas's mindsteps. His inset playlets are inherited from Douglas; so is his narrative waywardness, so too the outrageous *ex cathedra* pronouncements (if anything, the old Scot was even more of a tease). The diary *en plein air* had already been used by, among others, Edward Lear, to brilliant effect – 'I read and felt that I was there,' wrote Tennyson of the painter's Albanian journals. As for that rich vein of the absurd, it leads back via Lear to Laurence Sterne's *Sentimental Journey* and even earlier travellers: an exchange between Sykes and their light-fingered police escort near Tabriz – '"Are you a thief?" asked Christopher. "Yes I am," he replied' – took place in almost as many words over the border in Anatolia, in Ibn Battutah's fourteenth-century *Travels*.

The point is that, in Travel, nobody's his own forerunner. In Travel there's no *Ulysses*, no *Waste Land* – only Ulysses himself, and all the other travellers before and since, out there on the road, leading us through waste lands as yet unexplored. Some travellers, of course, are more visible than others. Robert Byron is one whose lead we cannot help but follow. He stands out above his generation, perhaps above all the travellers of the twentieth century. And this despite his all too short career: he died at 35, appropriately *en route*, on a ship torpedoed in the Mediterranean in 1941.

Seven years earlier, Byron had halted at an Afghan wayside shrine in a grove of umbrella-pines. In the way that smells do, their scent suddenly transported him back to another place – the Pinetum at Ravenna, which he visited on his first journey abroad. 'I might have been a dentist . . . but for that first sight of a larger world,' he wrote.

Thank goodness for Ravenna, and for all the other places that ravish us and set us on the road.

TIM MACKINTOSH-SMITH has always wanted to have a go at the prize suggested by Byron: '£10,000 for the first man to cover Marco Polo's outward route reading three fresh books a week, and another £10,000 if he drinks a bottle of wine a day as well. That man might tell one something about the journey.' Sadly, the prize was never endowed.

The drawings in this article appeared in letters Robert Byron wrote home while on his travels.

# *Blight, Mildew and Smut*

NICHOLAS MURRAY

One of the consequences of being Aldous Huxley's biographer was that I was invited to Eton, where a 17-year-old schoolboy with the bearing of a middle-aged barrister extended a hand and told me he had read *Crome Yellow* 'in my father's library'. In my mind's eye I saw a book-lined room opening on to a stone terrace in some country pile like the one in the novel. But then I remembered that the book had been written in a shady back street in the Tuscan seaside resort of Forte dei Marmi in the hot early summer of 1921.

*Crome Yellow* was the first of Huxley's novels I ever encountered. It never fails to brighten my spirits and is, I suspect, still read, while his more ambitious novels of the next decade, like *Point Counter Point* and *Eyeless in Gaza*, are gathering dust. When it first appeared at the start of the Roaring Twenties, bound between bright yellow boards, it made an immediate impact. Short, vivacious and terribly clever it was like being handed a glass of champagne which, ninety years on, is still fizzing.

The novel was greeted in the *Spectator* as 'a Cubist Peacock', a smart phrase that actually means little more than that it was modelled on the country-house novels of Thomas Love Peacock, *Headlong Hall* (1816) and *Nightmare Abbey* (1818), and that it was very modern. Huxley always privately thought of himself as an essayist and man of ideas rather than as a novelist, and the Peacockian novel was the perfect vehicle for a bright 27-year-old début writer to show

---

Aldous Huxley, *Crome Yellow* (1921)
Vintage · Pb · 192pp · £7.99 · ISBN 9780099461890

his skill. The *Times Literary Supplement* worried that 'he almost invites us to believe that the proper study of mankind is books', a very Huxleyan dilemma, but despite the fact that the novel has no particular plot to speak of – a young man on a bicycle arrives at a country house for the weekend, meets some clever and mad people, tries to fall in love, and goes home again – it manages to present a lively cast of eccentric characters who make it breathe and prevent its light Socratic elements from growing too serious. In fact, for all its showy displays of learning, and bits of Latin and French, it is quite free of any disabling gravitas.

The protagonist, Denis Stone, arrives at Crome after a hot July train journey through comically named English rustic halts, reflecting as he goes on the confusions of being young and ambitious for literary fame: 'He was twenty-three, and oh! so agonizingly conscious of the fact.' The prevailing tone of mockery alternating with youthful self-doubt will permeate all his observations and encounters at Crome, the grand house in the English countryside owned by Henry and Priscilla Wimbush, which has filled up for the weekend with painters, philosophers, playboys and unattached young women.

An early encounter occurs between Denis and the languidly knowing Anne, with whom he finds he is fruitlessly in love. He takes her into the garden and quotes Andrew Marvell at her, which provokes the retort: 'You have a bad habit of quoting . . . As I never know the context or author, I find it humiliating.'

Denis ruefully confesses, as one rather suspects Huxley was often forced to do, that this is 'the fault of one's education', and that he is intoxicated by words and by the literary associations that condition everything he sees. He is fully aware of this unwholesome obsession with books: 'One reads so many and one sees so few people and so little of the world.' He estimates that over the past five years he has read twenty or thirty tons of them.

Anne watches him striding up and down in front of the flowerbeds, expounding, as though she were at a lecture. 'He was a nice boy, and today he looked charming – charming!' He batters on with his complaint that Books are driving out Life: 'In the world of ideas everything was clear; in life all was obscure, embroiled. Was it surprising that one was miserable, horribly unhappy?' Anne thinks she quite admires his white flannel trousers.

Later, asked by a very earnest bluestocking to name the *crème de la crème* of the fashionable young poets, Denis replies languidly that his favourites are 'Blight, Mildew and Smut'.

Mr Scogan is another man of ideas whose set speeches about the Rational State, for example, are amusing lampoons on the progressive thought of the day. The shrill, mincing, 'old-maidish' voice in which these ideas are expounded calls to mind Bertrand Russell, and here we reach the *Crome Yellow* Problem. When she read the novel, Lady Ottoline Morrell was horrified. Huxley's spirited satire struck her as an unpardonable liberty. His cast of mad aristocrats, pontificating and life-hating vicars, priapic elder statesmen, comic gardeners, bohemian painters and batty spirit-world travellers were all drawn from life. Her life.

For whatever the architectural differences between Crome and Garsington Manor, whose hospitality Huxley had frequently enjoyed, the country house of the novel was obviously Lady Ottoline's Elizabethan manor in the Oxfordshire countryside at which, on a bicycle, Huxley had first arrived as a brilliant Balliol undergraduate in the autumn of 1915. If Scogan was loosely modelled on Russell, was not the bombastic painter Gombauld a little too reminiscent of Mark Gertler? Was not Jenny Mullion a little like Dorothy Brett and Mary Bracegirdle like Dorothy Carrington? The bon viveur Ivor Lombard immediately brought to mind the rich and pleasure-seeking philanderer Evan Morgan. But above all the hostess of Crome, Priscilla Wimbush, with her extravagant gowns, her over-the-top coiffure and 'mountainous orange head' was certainly the figure exhibited in Augustus John's scary canvas of Ottoline, now in the National Portrait Gallery, with its massive bonnet and beak-like nose.

Ottoline fired off an angry letter to Huxley, accusing him of making fun of the salty observations of the Garsington estate workers, of holding up the vicar's sermons to ridicule, and representing the former Prime Minister Herbert Asquith as 'an old man feebly toddling across the lawn after any pretty girl'. One has some sympathy with Ottoline, whose fate it has been to be satirized by the very people who had been recipients of her often enlightened and far-seeing patronage. She turns up in D. H. Lawrence's *Women in Love* as Hermione, as Lady Septuagesima in Osbert Sitwell's *Triple Fugue* (published three years after *Crome Yellow*) and in Gilbert Cannan's *Pugs and Peacocks*, published in 1921.

Aldous Huxley
by Mark Handley

In an extraordinarily disingenuous reply Huxley pretended to be astonished that anyone could possibly have discovered such correspondences between Garsington life and his 'little marionette performance', which was never intended to be taken as real. 'I ought to have laid the scene in China,' he protested. 'Nobody could have any doubt then that it was a marionette show.' He did concede that Denis was 'a caricature of myself in extreme youth', but he insisted that the remainder of the cast were 'puppets'. Then, with a candour of a kind more usual with him, he added that he actually had no wish, or even capacity, to represent real people, 'for I am not a realist, and don't take much interest in the problem of portraying real living people . . . the personages are just voices . . . They are puppets, devoid of all emotions.'

Huxley is too hard on himself, for if *Crome Yellow* were just a parade of cardboard characters enunciating all those beautifully polished parodic speeches the reader would quickly lose interest. What prevents that happening is the skill with which he brings to life an upper-middle-class English summer in 1920 still overshadowed by the recent Great War. The comic scenes and encounters – including some brilliant set-pieces like the tale of the ancestor of the house Sir Hercules, a dwarf who surrounds himself with people of restricted growth and hunts with pug dogs – are done with a consummately light and witty touch and are vividly dramatized and pictured: we can see the house, the characters sleeping on the leads in the moonlight, the bustle of the annual Crome Fair on the sloping lawns, the awkwardness and pain of young lovers, the clash of personalities and ideas at supper or in the breakfast room, the very English social comedy. Denis himself, and his tentativeness as he tries to come out of his protective shell and mingle with the crowds at the Bank Holiday Fair at Crome, is authentic and felt: 'His soul was a tenuous, tremulous, pale membrane. He would keep its sensibility intact and virgin as long as he could.'

At the end of the novel he engineers a spurious telegram that will call him away: 'It was an act performed, a decisive step taken – and he rarely took decisive steps.' It is a convincing portrait of a cerebral but hesitant and self-doubting youth trying to pick the lock of life, and Huxley knew that it was indeed 'a caricature of myself'.

NICHOLAS MURRAY's biography of Aldous Huxley (2002) has just been reprinted, as has a paperback edition of his book about the British poets of the Great War, *The Red Sweet Wine of Youth*. Born in Liverpool – the subject of his book *So Spirited a Town* – he divides his time between Bloomsbury and the Welsh Marches.

# *The Liquid Plains of the Sea*

ANDY MERRILLS

An enthusiastic bibliophile in a certain frame of mind could construct quite a library made up entirely of books that were written in prison. The poetry section would have the esoteric colour of *Le Morte d'Arthur* and Ezra Pound's *Pisan Cantos*; political thought would be unusually well stocked, with *The Consolation of Philosophy* and *The Prince* vying for attention with Gramsci's *Prison Notebooks*; and those with an off-beat sense of humour might enjoy the juxtaposition of John Bunyan's *Pilgrim's Progress* with John Cleland's *Fanny Hill*. For me, though, the particular highlight of the library would be the history section, in which pride of place would certainly be granted to Fernand Braudel's monumental work *The Mediterranean and the Mediterranean World in the Age of Philip II* (1949).

For several decades after the Second World War, Braudel was unquestionably the most prominent historian in France, but it was while he was interned after his capture by German troops in 1940 that he drafted the work for which he will always be remembered. Written without his notes or access to any reference works, *The Mediterranean* was not only a genuinely beautiful paean to a disappearing world, it also represented a whole new template for historical and geographical scholarship.

---

Fernand Braudel, *The Mediterranean and the Mediterranean World in the Age of Philip II* (1949), 3 vols. Only the first two volumes in an English translation are still in print, as paperbacks from the University of California Press: Vol. 1 · 642pp · £30.95 · ISBN 9780520203089; Vol. 2 · 726pp · £30.95 · ISBN 9780520203303.
Henri Pirenne, *Mohammed and Charlemagne* (1937), is out of print in English.

Braudel's ostensible concern was to compose a coherent interpretation of Spanish history in the late sixteenth century – a golden age for the Iberian peninsula, but one in which its destiny was inextricably bound to the great inland sea to the east. To do this, the historian consciously turned away from the personalities and battles that had long dominated the histories of the period; these were, as he saw it, little more than the cresting whitecaps on the tides of history. Instead, he focused on the swells of the waves themselves and the deep but inexorable currents beneath, on the seemingly eternal rhythms of economic and social life, and on the ways in which the landscape of the Mediterranean world had shaped the lives of those many people who had lived on its shores since the time of Homer.

Braudel helped to take the individual out of history, but his *Mediterranean* is still crowded with people, and it is this which makes it such a pleasure to read. By shifting focus away from Philip II, Suleiman the Magnificent and innumerable angry popes who had jealously jostled for position in traditional historiography, Braudel made room for those actors who would otherwise barely feature on the stage. For him, true Mediterranean history was about the perennial shuttling of coastal traders from port to port (and their regrettable tendency to turn to piracy when things got tricky), the invisible threads that bound the great coastal cities of the sea to one another, and the respiratory rhythms that lifted mountain-dwellers up to the highland pastures to graze their flocks, and then drew them down to the market and to the curious gaze of history. For Braudel, it was the countless figures in their landscape who were the true actors in history, and this history was often unchanging. As Siân Reynolds's wonderful English translation puts it:

> The vast low-lying plain of the Sienese Maremma, a real fever trap, is, like its neighbour the Tuscan Maremma, dotted with noblemen's castles. Their anachronistic silhouettes of tower and keep conjure up a whole society, the crushing presence of the

> feudal landlords who dominated the country without even living there, for these residences were only their temporary abodes. Most of the year the masters lived in Siena, in the huge town houses still standing today, palaces into which Bandello's lovers find their way, with the ritual complicity of the servants, up staircases leading to the great attics where stacks of grain are stored, or along corridors leading to the rooms on the ground floor, always a little neglected. We can follow them into the houses of these old families to relive the comedies and tragedies whose dénouement would take place in secret in the old castle in Maremma, far from town gossip and family control. Isolated from the world by fever and sultry heat, what better place could there be for putting to death, according to the custom of Italy and the century, an unfaithful wife – or one suspected of being so?

Braudel's conviction that individuals' actions were determined by their context – that history was shaped by geography – sculpted the very structure of *The Mediterranean* itself. The first of the three volumes, and certainly the most widely read, is essentially a human geography of the Mediterranean, its islands, coastlines, tributary rivers and mountainous fringes. Here, Braudel's sun-drenched (and occasionally snow-flecked) prose combines with the sumptuous illustrations of many modern editions to create what is effectively a sensitive travelogue of the great inland sea.

The second volume of *The Mediterranean* is concerned with what Braudel terms 'collective destinies'. This is the history of changing economic systems and the rise and fall of the great sea-borne empires – narratives that long outlasted the lifetime of an individual merchant or prince, but which might recognizably adapt and change over decades if not centuries. Here, the historian moves away from the travelogue, but not from its breadth of interest. And, crucially, the work remains resolutely a human history: 'These apparently trivial details', Braudel says, 'tell us more than any formal description about the life of a Mediterranean man – a wandering life, tossed in every direction by the winds of fortune.' Thus we read of the growth of Venetian trade or the ubiquity of Jewish diaspora communities through the experiences of individuals. Invariably, these slender threads of anecdotal evidence are pulled together brilliantly, as in Braudel's assessment of the endemic piracy of the Mediterranean (perhaps my favourite chapter of the whole work):

> All, from the most wretched to the most powerful, rich and poor alike, cities, lords and states were caught up in a web of operations cast over the whole sea. In the past, western historians have encouraged us to see only the pirates of Islam, in particular the Barbary corsairs. The notorious fortune of Algiers tends to blind one to the rest. But this fortune is not unique; Malta and Leghorn were Christendom's Algiers, they too had their bagnios, their slave markets and their sordid transactions . . .

It is only in the final volume of *The Mediterranean* that Braudel turns directly to the age of Philip II. Predictably, this is probably the least read section of the history but it is still emphatically a work of startling historical scholarship. Here, Braudel is concerned with the struggle between the Spanish King and the Ottoman Sultan, Suleiman the Magnificent, during the middle decades of the sixteenth century. This was a conflict that raged from Vienna to Algiers and included the great siege of Malta in 1565. The struggle came to a head in 1571 in the Battle of Lepanto when, in G. K. Chesterton's words more than three centuries later, 'the inmost sea of all the earth is shaken with his ships'. Lepanto was the last of the great clashes of Mediterranean galleys, and occupies a central position in innumerable military and naval histories; Braudel's great accomplishment was to see this, not simply as a second Actium, or as a chapter in a sixteenth-century 'clash of civilizations', but as one small wave in a great, organic sea.

Braudel's *Mediterranean* would not be the only work of history in the prisoners' library. By strange coincidence another great study of the Mediterranean, by another great Francophone scholar, was drafted in strikingly similar circumstances twenty years earlier. Between 1916 and 1918, the Belgian historian Henri Pirenne laid out the plan of his *Mohammed and Charlemagne* in another German prisoner-of-war camp. Pirenne's volume is rather slighter than those of Braudel, and lacks the latter's sumptuous prose, but it too had a profound influence upon generations of historians, and it too allowed its author an imaginative escape from the grim realities of a restricted world. Ultimately it is this fabulous capacity for imaginative escapism that makes Braudel's *Mediterranean* such a delight. And to judge from the author's own preface, he was well aware of this too:

> I have loved the Mediterranean with a passion, no doubt because I am a northerner like so many others in whose footsteps I have followed. I have joyfully dedicated long years of study to it – much more than all my youth. In return, I hope that a little of this joy and a great deal of Mediterranean sunlight will shine from the pages of this book. Ideally perhaps one should, like the novelist, have one's subject under control, never losing it from sight and constantly aware of its overpowering presence. Fortunately or unfortunately, the historian has not the novelist's freedom. The reader who approaches this book in the spirit I would wish will do well to bring with him his own memories, his own vision of the Mediterranean to add colour to the text and to help me conjure up this vast presence, as I have done my best to do.

ANDY MERRILLS teaches Ancient History at the University of Leicester. For one term as an undergraduate, he tried to write all his essays in the style of Fernand Braudel. He now remembers this with some embarrassment.

# *A Term at Haggard Hall*

ANTHONY GARDNER

Over the years I have been sent many proof copies of books, but very few that I have bothered to keep. They are, in general, unattractive creatures, with their misprints and vainglorious boasts of future bestsellerdom. But in a corner of an attic shelf I have half a dozen which seem too interesting to throw away, and chief among them is Nicholas Best's *Tennis and the Masai*. The mere sight of its dog-eared, pale green cover – embellished only by the Hutchinson logo, with its curious resemblance to a buffalo's skull – is enough to lift my spirits.

Published in 1986, this story of a Kenyan prep school is very much in the tradition of Evelyn Waugh – but where so many writers have offered poor imitations, Best shows a lightness of touch and zest for invention that mark him as a master of comedy in his own right.

He is quick to acknowledge his debt: one of the book's epigraphs is from Waugh's *Remote People*, and *Black Mischief* is mentioned on the second page. The opening scene is a reworking of that of *Decline and Fall*, with two figures in authority commenting on the wild behaviour of a group of revellers – but there is a twist. The pair taking tea at the Mombasa Club are not old colonials but Mr District Commander Karanja and Mr bin Seyd, the superintendent of police; the naked bacchants are German holidaymakers frolicking on the beach.

> 'A pastoral people in their way,' observed Karanja. 'One can't expect them to change overnight. They're tourists, after all . . . There are times, you know, when I envy them their simplicity.'

---

Nicholas Best, *Tennis and the Masai* (1986), is out of print.

The conversation turns to Karanja's family. His younger boy is at Haggard Hall, 'an exclusive establishment to which all the aristocratic settlers sent their sons'. In a skilful, filmic transition, Karanja's attention is caught by the chuntering of the night train to Nairobi:

> Towards the same time tomorrow – assuming no elephants on the line, locusts in the engine, floods, bush fires or even *shauri ya Mungu*, the will of God – the train would be approaching Naivasha, six thousand feet up in what had once been the White Highlands; and Stephen Karanja would hear it in the distance, as his father heard it now.

Haggard Hall is a baronial mansion built by an ill-fated member of the Happy Valley set (the subject of Best's first, non-fiction book) within sight of Mount Longonot, the extinct volcano which partly inspired Rider Haggard's *She*. The addition of barbed-wire fences and watchtowers during the Mau Mau uprising has given the school the appearance of an upmarket concentration camp. Presiding over it is Desmond Gale, a former soldier and professional gambler who – after one narrow squeak too many – has opted for a life of relative respectability. The other members of the academic staff are Eugene Nodleman, a would-be anthropologist whose credulity is endlessly exploited by the local tribesmen, and the Padre, who has long forgotten his reasons for taking holy orders and devotes himself to breeding carrier pigeons.

What the school lacks is a maths teacher. Desmond likes the idea of a military man; the nearest he can find is Martin Riddle, a recent graduate hoping to make a career in the Royal Army Educational Corps. Turned down by Sandhurst, Martin has been advised to reapply in nine months and 'get his knees brown' in the meantime.

Martin is as wet behind the ears as they come. Brought up in suburban Purley Way, his only trip abroad has been to France; his mother still packs his suitcase and buys his underwear. His status as a tenderfoot is symbolized by the bush hat with a fake leopard-skin ribbon that she foists upon him – but no sooner has he stepped off the train at Naivasha than his passage to manhood begins. His first task is to join the hunt for Smith-Baggot, a 12-year-old serial runner-away trying to make his way home across the 13,000-foot Aberdare Mountains. His second is to oversee the school's Guy Fawkes celebrations, during which he accidentally inspires a Somali groundsman – frustrated by his wife's puritanical attitude to sex – to take revenge on the neighbouring Catholic mission. Other notable events during Martin's tenure include a run-in with a hungry leopard and a cricket match at which the Padre's pigeons come into their own.

Some of these ingredients, the notes on the back cover tell me, derive from Nicholas Best's own experience as a pupil at a Kenyan school during the 1950s. His tale is updated to the 1980s, with Martin's soldierly instincts stirred by the Falklands crisis – but while the political map of Africa has been redrawn, attitudes remain largely unchanged. The spirit of the colonial past is embodied by Lady Bullivant, a daughter of the Raj who teaches riding at the school and thinks nothing of castrating a stallion before breakfast:

> It was said of her, and no one doubted it, that when Mau Mau terrorists had rustled cattle from her farm, she had personally tracked down the culprits at the head of a Masai war party and supervised their annihilation. She was one of those settlers who never locked a door during the Emergency, so terrified were the natives of what she might do to them.

Clearly none of the staff is better qualified to lead the hunt for a troublesome leopard. When it kills and partially devours the groundsman's son, Lady Bullivant pooh-poohs the idea of burial and insists that the remains must be dosed with strychnine and left out to tempt the returning predator.

Most of the book's humour is in a lighter vein. There is a good running joke about a flamingo which Smith-Baggot first befriends and then eats, with unfortunate results; the headmaster – a keen fisherman – is later found using its feathers to make flies. It is the Padre's pigeons, though, that give wings to the author's imagination as he explores their emotions with gentle anthropomorphism. The pride of the loft, Siege of Paris, is ruthlessly prepared for a vital mission – carrying the score from a cricket match against a distant school – by introducing him to a seductive mate who is then snatched away. As the team sets off, a rival male is added to the equation:

> The hen bird preened happily. Siege of Paris goggled through the bars and fought to escape. This perfidy of womankind was new to him . . .
>
> 'That should do it,' the Padre thought. He allowed Siege of Paris one last, despairing glance. The hen continued to flaunt herself. Siege of Paris struggled against the bars, imploring her to reconsider. His fellow inmates gave him their sympathy. A rumble of disapproval arose and showed no sign of abating as the Padre loaded them into the minibus.

As for the pupils of Haggard Hall, they carry on in the manner of schoolboys everywhere, with small local variations. When Fife-Nugent is given a hundred lines, it is to write 'No tarantulas in class'; his classmate Nightshade is discovered with a pot of honey in his hand trying to lure a column of safari ants into the staff room.

Best only occasionally pauses to describe the African bush, but when he does it is with a deft lyrical touch: 'They drove along the lake road, through a herd of Thomson's gazelle grazing illicitly at the edge of the papyrus. A fish eagle hung mutely in the warm air, behind it a pair of pelicans. The umbrella trees formed a broad swathe of yellow against the blue depths of the water.'

Like Laurel and Hardy before him, Best recognizes the comic mileage to be had from incompetence. Eugene Nodleman's dealings with the Masai are a case in point: though he fantasizes about making headlines as an outsider welcomed into the tribe, he is actually no nearer than the average tourist to discovering their secrets.

Meanwhile Martin, as the only person at the school who does not know how to drive, suffers the indignity of being chauffeured by one of his 12-year-old pupils.

Unusually, though, Best recognizes the flipside of this: the enjoyment that derives from a show of competence, particularly by someone of whom it is not expected. Who could help but admire Smith-Baggot as he methodically prepares for his first escape attempt?

Daniel Macklin

He was a resourceful boy, small for his age but determined. He had already gathered his equipment for the expedition – a compass, a waterproof torch, and a bush knife which he had used to cut the throat of a Thomson's gazelle which had unwisely strayed across the school boundary at the bottom of the playing fields. The Tommy would provide all the food he needed for the trip. After hanging the carcass to drain the blood, he had sliced the flesh into long strips to dry in the sun.

It is Martin's progress from ineptitude to competence, culminating in a triumphant return to the Army Commissions Board, that gives this delightful book its shape. It would be wrong to suggest that *Tennis and the Masai* is a challenger to *Black Mischief* as the best comic novel written about Africa, but it does offer an unflagging sense of fun, and something that Waugh in his cynicism was never eager to give his readers: a really satisfying ending.

ANTHONY GARDNER has never been to Kenya, though he once slept in the world's smallest tent in Botswana. Nor is he much good at tennis, though he loves it. He edits the Royal Society of Literature *Review*, and is the author of a novel, *The Rivers of Heaven.*

# *Fitting Memorials*

ARIANE BANKES

As soon as I could hold a pen I was taught copperplate script by my splendidly bossy elder sister, who was determined to pre-empt any teacher's pernicious influence. I can still remember the thrill of achieving an infant version of that delicate balance between broad sweep and fine line, of swooping between upper and lower registers, creating delicious patterns on the page that actually meant something. From that promising start my handwriting has deteriorated steadily over the decades, but friends say they still see some trace of its origins, and one legacy of that early tuition is my lifelong love of lettering. As teenagers we biked around East Anglian churches with tubes of paper and blocks of wax crayon poking out of our baskets, alighting to tease out vigorous impressions of ancient brasses in dusty naves, the curlicues of their script imperfectly ghosting through the paper, and I have haunted country graveyards with their slanting stones and lichened legends ever since.

Imagine my pleasure then when, on a recent visit to Blair Castle in Perthshire, I came across two elegant inscriptions from Milton's *Paradise Lost* on Purbeck stone standing sentinel either side of a gateway; inside, dotted around the walled Hercules Garden, stood further beautifully executed examples of lettered stone bearing their lines of consolation or celebration: Julian of Norwich's elegaic 'All shall be well' picking up the light from the morning sun in its jagged runnel of gold; Charlotte Howarth's wry 'Remember Me' raising a rueful smile from passers-by. Here is just a selection of the Art and Memory Collection originally commissioned by the Memorial Arts Charity (now renamed The Lettering and Commemorative Arts

Trust, or LCAT), which is scattered across various sites in Britain as a reminder of how beautiful and varied memorial art can be.

It is all the inspiration of Harriet Frazer who, in the 1980s, frustrated in her search for a memorial for her stepdaughter Sophie Behrens, founded Memorials by Artists, dedicated to revitalizing the art of stone letter-cutting and thereby providing an eloquent channel for the articulation of memory and grief. So I set out to Suffolk to find out more about this remarkable venture.

Arriving at Snape Priory, I was directed down a drive through woodland which shelters more standing stones, to a Victorian country house with a pastoral view over Suffolk cornfields, where I was greeted warmly by Harriet and her husband Simon. Harriet is the daughter of Heywood and Anne Hill, founder-proprietors of the eponymous bookshop in Mayfair and sometime employers of Nancy Mitford, among others. It was Anne Hill's mother Dorothy Cranbrook who bought Snape Priory in 1926, and the house seems delightfully arrested in time, with faded paintwork and a dashing portrait by Oliver Messel of the young Heywood Hill hanging in the hall. The charity is run from converted outbuildings, from which Harriet and her tiny staff manage an ever-spreading network of creative collaborations involving seventy craftsmen (and women), one that is gently transforming the landscape of commemoration.

It all started simply: 'The idea came so suddenly,' she admits, 'I can remember the very spot on the road.' Her stepdaughter's death was the catalyst; she found herself fruitlessly battling churchyard rules and regulations in an effort to create a memorial that would do Sophie's young life justice – and even when she found a sculptor to help, they

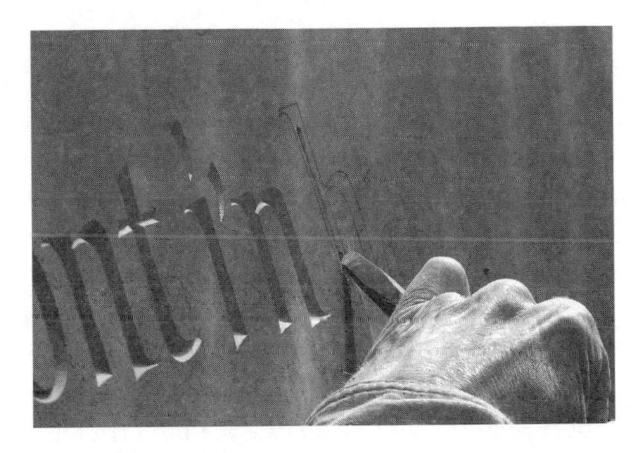

were prevented by sheer bureaucracy from using the lines of poetry that they wanted. Two years of dogged persistence paid off eventually in achieving a uniquely beautiful headstone for Sophie, and every thing stemmed from there.

As always when you look into a hitherto unexplored subject, it turns out to be infinitely more complex than you had ever imagined. I had been under the illusion that letter-carvers use and adapt existing fonts, but even a brief walk round the grounds of Snape Priory showed how mistaken I was. No two memorials look remotely the same. There is an endless variety – not just of stone (or wood) and shape, but of form and flow and heft and weight in the letters employed. Each letter-carver seems to reinvent the wheel, responding intuitively to the sense and sensibility of the words that he is bringing to life with his chisel. And even if an existing letterform is loosely followed, no two letters are ever the same: for all the precision and accuracy of the carver, minute variations will creep in to distinguish one from another.

Harriet's garden serves a practical purpose, too: potential clients often visit Snape Priory to wander around and see what's possible, to give them ideas and to judge what they do and don't like, before taking the plunge. There are also the questions of how to locate a sympathetic carver; how to decide on the type of stone or wood; what text to choose; how to navigate your way through the church's regulations, if a graveyard is in your sights – on all of which LCAT advises. Indeed the crux of their work is introducing client to carver for what will be a critical collaboration, for deep feelings are involved in commissioning any memorial, and nerves can get very frayed if things go wrong.

Do they ever go wrong, I wonder. 'Well, they can,' Harriet admits. 'There was an awful time when I was rung up on holiday by a distraught and very-much-alive client who had just taken delivery of a stone with both her name and that of her recently deceased husband inscribed on it. Needless to say there had been a misunderstanding, and hers was supposed to go on later. She was furious, and the whole stone had to be redone without her name – at some expense to the artist . . .' Luckily, such misadventures are rare.

And where do all these letter-carvers learn their craft? It's incredibly skilled work, tough, arduous and often solitary, and not an obvious road to riches. The earlier generation of craftsmen is slowly dwindling, and Harriet is determined to maintain and renew the tradition by raising funds for two-year apprenticeships, as well as running short courses in letter-carving all over the country. Initially it was difficult to find professional carvers willing and able to afford an apprentice, so they are given a grant towards expenses, as is the student. Six of these have now finished their training and have set out on their own.

Among them is Stuart Buckle, who trained with the Norfolk-based letter artist Gary Breeze before going it alone five years ago. His commissions have ranged from standing stones at Eton College and a memorial on London's Horse Guards' Parade to a commemoration for the victims of the Bali bombing, garden plaques and headstones for pets. It's an uncertain life, pulling out all the stops at one moment to meet a deadline, scraping around for work the next, but he seems happy with what it offers: independence, variety, the sense of creating something that will last 'much, much longer than you will, and might even outlive you by centuries'. The intrinsic satisfaction of

Engraving on glass by Bettina Furnée, St John's Church, Snape

fashioning a thing of beauty with patience and skill more than compensates for the loneliness of the job.

Carving, ultimately, can be a meditative pursuit: the close focus on words and feelings and their transformation into physical form demands expertise laced with empathy, an imaginative mind and a deft and steady hand. And the result is an object of beauty that stops us in our tracks and effectively earths us, cutting through the busyness of our lives to remind us of evanescence, of love and loss, perhaps of hope and renewal, too.

ARIANE BANKES helps to run various festivals when not wishing she had the time, talent and patience to retrain as a letter-carver.

For more details on The Lettering and Commemorative Arts Trust (LCAT), see www.memorialsbyartists.co.uk and www.memorialartscharity.org.uk. The Trust will be displaying its work, with demonstrations of letter-carving and works for sale, at Art in Action, Waterperry, Oxfordshire, 19–22 July 2012.

# *Bibliography*


Nicholas Best, *Tennis and the Masai* 84

Ahmed Hassanein Bey, *The Lost Oases* 19

Fernand Braudel, *The Mediterranean and the Mediterranean World in the Age of Philip II* 79

Anthony Burgess, *Inside Mr Enderby*; *Enderby Outside*; *The Clockwork Testament, or Enderby's End*; *Enderby's Dark Lady, or No End of Enderby* 50

Robert Byron, *The Road to Oxiana* 68

C. A. Gibson-Hill, *British Sea Birds*; *Birds of the Coast* 35

Kenneth Grahame, *The Wind in the Willows* 7

William Hickey, *Memoirs of a Georgian Rake* 58

Aldous Huxley, *Crome Yellow* 74

Elspeth Huxley, *The Flame Trees of Thika* 14

Jan Karon, *At Home in Mitford*; *A Light in the Windows*; *These High, Green Hills*; *Out to Canaan*; *A New Song*; *A Common Life*; *In This Mountain*; *Shepherds Abiding*; *Light from Heaven*; *In the Company of Others* 64

The Lettering and Commemorative Arts Trust 89

Fergus Linnane, *London: The Wicked City* 58

The London Library 45

Horace McCoy, *They Shoot Horses, Don't They?* 24

Henri Pirenne, *Mohammed and Charlemagne* 79

Peter Russell, *The Elegies of Quintilius* 29

John Kennedy Toole, *A Confederacy of Dunces* 40

# Coming attractions . . .

CHRISTIAN TYLER receives a late education

KATE MACDONALD meets a good comrade

RICHARD KNOTT sets sail with Arthur Ransome

JUDY SPOURS takes lessons from Mrs Beeton

DAVID SPILLER goes to Downing Street

BEN WHITROW remembers Denton Welch

YSENDA MAXTONE GRAHAM finds a catcher in the rye

RICHARD PLATT settles in a quiet neighbourhood